THE GREAT COMPOSERS
THEIR LIVES AND TIMES

Edward
Elgar
1857-1934

Richard
Strauss
1864-1949

Gustav
Holst
1874-1934

Joaquín
Rodrigo
b.1901

THE GREAT COMPOSERS
THEIR LIVES AND TIMES

Edward

Elgar
1857-1934

Richard

Strauss
1864-1949

Gustav

Holst
1874-1934

Joaquín

Rodrigo
b.1901

MARSHALL CAVENDISH
NEW YORK · LONDON · SYDNEY

Staff Credits

Editors
Laura Buller
David Buxton

Art Editors
Helen James
Debbie Jecock

Deputy Editor
Barbara Segall

Sub-editors
Geraldine Jones
Judy Oliver
Nigel Rodgers

Designers
Steve Chilcott
Shirin Patel
Chris Rathbone

Picture Researchers
Georgina Barker
Julia Calloway
Vanessa Cawley

Production Controllers
Deborah Cracknell
Sue Fuller

Secretary
Lynn Small

Publishing Director
Reg Wright

Managing Editor
Sue Lyon

Consultants
Dr Antony Hopkins
Commander of the Order
of the British Empire
Fellow of the
Royal College of Music

Nick Mapstone BA, MA

Keith Shadwick BA

Reference Edition Published 1990

Published by Marshall Cavendish Corporation
147 West Merrick Road
Freeport, Long Island
N.Y. 11520

Typeset by Maclink, Hull
Printed by Times Offset Private Ltd.,
Singapore

© Marshall Cavendish Limited MCMLXXXIV,
MCMLXXXVII, MCMXC
Library of Congress Cataloging-in-Publication Data

The Composers: the great composers, their lives and times.
*   p. ca.*
*   Cover title: Great composers II.*
*   ISBN 1-85435-300-4 (set): $175.00*
*   1. Composers—Biography.   2. Music appreciation.*
I. Marshall Cavendish Corporation.
II. Title: Great composers II.
ML390.C7185 1990   780'.92'2—dc20 [B]   89-23988

ISBN 1-85435-300-4 (set)   CIP
*   1-85435-304-7 (vol)   MN*

THE
GREAT COMPOSERS
THEIR LIVES AND TIMES

Contents

Introduction

The early years of the 20th century saw startling developments in every facet of society. Landmarks in science, medicine, transport and technology brought about an era of change perhaps more profound than any other in history. In addition, the advent of mass communications greatly accelerated the impact of these landmarks; those living in priviliged countries were swept into a new era of technology.

Not surprisingly, Europe's new technological image was reflected in the arts of the first 30 years of the century. Painters, writers, poets and composers, sensitive to the changes around them, showed in their respective work all the symptoms of a culture in rapid transition. The works of the four composers found in this volume helped to create a bridge between established musical traditions and modern music.

Edward Elgar's rich, melodic masterpieces rightly belonged to the great European tradition. His role in reviving English music's international reputation paved the way for modern English composers.

Richard Strauss's best works convey the complexities of human feeling in a realistic manner. As both a composer and a conductor, he remains a pivotal figure.

Gustav Holst found influence in both the English Romantic movement and in international developments, giving his music a sophisticated appeal. His visionary teaching skills left a firm impression on music education.

Joaquín Rodrigo's colourful concertos for guitar evoke the traditional music of his native Spain. Yet his music is not simply a nostalgic look back; it has broadly advanced the use of guitar in the modern classical repertory.

THE GREAT COMPOSERS

Edward Elgar

1857–1934

Edward Elgar was born in a small village and had almost no formal musical education, yet he became the pre-eminent British composer of the early 20th century. His achievements helped to re-establish the reputation of English music. When his masterful oratorio The Dream of Geronitus was performed in Germany, Richard Strauss fêted Elgar as 'the first English progressive composer'. His gifts of melody and strong sense of Romantic traditions lent his works immediate popular appeal. Two of his compositions, the intriguing Enigma Variations and the rousing Pomp and Circumstance Marches, are analysed in the Listener's Guide. The unequivocal Englishness of Elgar's music captures the feel and spirit of a nation in its heyday as an imperial world power; British rule in India became the very symbol of its power, as In The Background *describes.*

As a young man in Worcester in rural England, Elgar had ambitions far beyond those of a talented local musician and teacher. Determined to expand upon his regional reputation, he and his wife moved to London in 1889; ironically, it was on their return to the countryside that Elgar began to achieve recognition with his cantatas. However, it was his orchestral work, Enigma Variations, which consolidated his fame. For the next two decades, Elgar was at the peak of his creativity and success. The composer whom critics had once called 'provincial' had now been knighted, had received honorary degrees from Oxford and Yale Universities, and had seen one of the tunes from his Pomp and Circumstance marches rival the British national anthem in popularity. Although he felt out of touch during his last years and produced no major works, Elgar had already paved the way for the generation of English composers to follow.

COMPOSER'S LIFE
'English progressive'

Edward Elgar rose from humble provincial origins to gain a knighthood for his services to music. He also became the first English composer in 200 years to win international acclaim.

Edward Elgar was born at Broadheath, just outside Worcester, England, in 1857. His father, William Elgar, originally from Dover, had settled in Worcester in 1841, and with his brother set up in business as a piano-tuner and music retailer. He was also organist of St George's Catholic Church, and some of Edward's earliest musical experiences were gained watching his father at work in the organ loft. His mother, Anne Elgar, was a well-read woman from whom he derived his background in literature.

When Edward was nearly three the family moved into Worcester, where they lived above the music shop – Elgar Brothers, at 10 High Street. Edward, however, often returned to Broadheath in his school holidays and came to know and love this part of the countryside. This love of rural surroundings was to stay with him for the rest of his life and was to make its way into much of his music.

Apart from the valuable musical background at home, Elgar had very little formal musical education

– in fact, he was largely self-taught. He played both the piano and the violin, and at one point had ambitions to study at the famous Leipzig Conservatoire. Unfortunately, when he left school in 1872, aged 15, his family could not afford to send him. His parents, knowing that the life of a professional musician could be insecure, proposed instead that he became articled in a solicitor's office. After a year he persuaded his parents that this was not where his ambition lay and, consequently, he was released from his articles. The business experience, however, was not wasted – he began to help with the accounts of the family shop where he had access to a wealth of music. He also began giving violin lessons and gradually built up a local reputation as teacher, performer, arranger and, on occasion, composer.

In 1877 he spent twelve days in London, taking a short course of lessons to improve his playing, with Adolphe Pollitzer, leader of the New Philharmonic Orchestra. Pollitzer, was impressed by his young pupil and urged him to return for further instruction, but Elgar eventually decided against a virtuoso performance career, feeling that his tone was too thin.

From 1879 he was a member, and later conductor, of the Worcester Glee Club. He also played the

Edward Elgar was born on 2 June 1857 in the cottage at Broadheath (above left). In 1860 the family returned to Worcester to live above Elgar Brothers shop at No 10, High Street (below). Elgar grew up there and with his family took part in the provincial but not insubstantial musical life of the Cathedral city of Worcester (above). Although he sought musical recognition beyond his home front he was always at his most creative when close to his beloved Malverns – the hills close to the city.

Up to this point most of what Elgar had composed was so-called 'salon music', and although he believed himself capable of greater things, his powers of more extended musical thought and composition had yet to be exercised. But during these early years he came into contact with the music of composers such as Wagner and Schumann who were to exert considerable influence upon him. In 1882 he spent three weeks in Leipzig where he attended the Opera and heard the famous Gewandhaus Orchestra.

In 1884, the Three Choirs Festival held in Worcester coincided with the 800th anniversary of Worcester Cathedral, and the celebration included a visit by Dvořák, who conducted his *Stabat Mater* and his *D Major Symphony* (now known as No. 6). Elgar, who played in the violins at the festival was enthralled by Dvořák's music.

The following year, 1885, brought the satisfaction of seeing his music in print for the first time, with the publication of violin pieces first by John Beare, then by Schott's. Also in that year he was appointed organist of St George's, succeeding his father who had retired.

Marriage to Alice Roberts

Among his many lady pupils was Caroline Alice Roberts, the only daughter of an Indian Army Major-General, Sir Henry Gee Roberts. When she began lessons, in October 1886, she was already 38 and, since the death of her father and the departure of her brothers to the Army, she had remained at home to look after her mother. She was a cultivated woman, with an interest in music which extended to singing in the local choir. The choir was often accompanied

bassoon in a wind quintet (which also included his oboist brother Frank) and during 1879–84 coached, played in and later conducted, the band at the County Lunatic Asylum at Powick – where the Superintendent had progressive ideas about the beneficial effects of music on his patients. In 1882 he became first violin in W. C. Stockley's Orchestra in Birmingham – Stockley's Popular Concerts were an established and well known feature of Midland musical life.

Early ambitions

Busy as he was, Elgar cherished ambitions far beyond those of a talented local musician. In any time that he was not conducting, performing or teaching he was composing, or listening to other people's work. He spent much of his earnings from teaching the violin and piano to the young ladies of Worcester and Malvern on travelling to London to hear August Manns' famous concerts at Crystal Palace. Manns, a German conductor was music director at the Crystal Palace and was responsible for providing good music at popular prices. Elgar's ambition to be recognized beyond his local boundaries had its first realization in July 1884 when the score of an orchestral work, *Sevillana,* shown by Elgar to Politzer, was sent to Manns, who included it in one of his Concerts.

Elgar wrote his early compositions for the woodwind quintet (right) which he formed together with three friends and his brother Frank. They are, from left to right, standing – William Leicester (clarinet), Edward Elgar (bassoon), Hubert Leicester (flute), and seated, Frank Exton (flute) and Frank Elgar (oboe).

by a string orchestra in which Elgar played. In 1887 Lady Roberts died and Alice, inheriting a small income, moved from the family home to lodgings in Malvern Link near Worcester. Her friendship with Edward prospered but when a year later their engagement was announced her aunts and cousins expressed strongly their disapproval of her involvement with a tradesman's son.

Regardless of the opposition, Alice and Edward were married in May 1889 at the Brompton Oratory in London; soon after they took up residence in London – moving first to Kensington, then Norwood and finally back to Kensington again. Both felt that London was the place to be to win the wider recognition he sought, since London was where the publishers and music promoters were based. With Alice's income to fall back on Elgar was able to devote more time and energy to composing and to keeping abreast of musical developments in the capital city. He did, however, return to Malvern once a week to fulfil teaching commitments.

In terms of publishing Elgar scored a notable success with a small piano piece called *Liebesgrüss* (Love's greeting), which was published by Schott under the title *Salut d'Amour*. It earned a great deal for the publisher but, unfortunately, Elgar had sold the manuscript outright and therefore had no financial share in its success. Although Manns performed *Salut d'Amour* and the *Suite in D* at Crystal Palace, wider public recognition of his own work remained elusive.

Family life in London was made happier by the arrival of their only child, Carice, in March 1890, but apart from this life in the city was not living up to the expectations Elgar had of it. City life also aggravated his health – he was susceptible to throat trouble throughout his life. Furthermore, neither commissions nor pupils were arriving in quantity as he hoped they would. It was decided that the family would return to Malvern where at least Elgar could earn a living as a teacher and compose at the same time. So, in June 1891, the Elgars moved back to Malvern.

Elgar and Caroline Alice Roberts (above left) were married in May 1889 despite great opposition from Alice's family, who felt that she was marrying beneath herself. Her love for Elgar lies behind the creation of most of his masterpieces, including The Dream of Gerontius *(final page of the score shown above). After her death Elgar produced no original work of any note.*

Return to the provinces

Finding himself in the round of teaching the violin to young ladies again, Elgar was naturally despondent, but in reality the return to Malvern was probably fortunate. Although publishers and critics were in London, the heart of English musical life was, at that time, to be found in the great oratorio festivals, in Leeds, Birmingham, Sheffield and cities which hosted the Three Choirs – Worcester, Gloucester and Hereford.

During the 1890s Elgar produced several cantatas – including *The Black Knight* and *Scenes from the Saga of King Olaf,* both inspired by works of the American poet Longfellow, a love of whose work he shared with his mother, and *Caractacus.* Back in his beloved Malvern Hills and surrounded by many friends it seemed that he had found the milieu that suited his creative impulse.

Elgar at last began to be rewarded with some measure of recognition. His works were greatly appreciated by those who performed them and, even if some critics continued to write patronizingly of him as a 'provincial' composer, the more enterprising conductors of the choral societies in the Midlands and the North began to show interest in his work and put on their own performances of it.

In 1897 the organizers of the Leeds Festival, then the leading platform for English composers, gave him a commission. Although Elgar would have preferred to write a symphony it was a cantata which they required. The result was *Caractacus* – a story of Britons and Romans, set in Elgar's Malvern Hills. Everything augured well for the first performance – Queen Victoria had accepted Elgar's dedication of the work to her and the first-night audience included

Elgar began work on what he planned to be a symphony in 1901, but the result was a concert overture, Cockaigne (In London Town), *(title page above). This was a series of variations inspired by the sights and sounds of London (left) – the city to which he had often travelled to attend concerts and hear new music.*

many celebrities, among them the French composer Gabriel Fauré, and many of Elgar's close friends. However, the performance was not as good as it might have been, and the critics concluded, once again, that Elgar was an up-and-coming composer, rather than one who had created a masterpiece.

Friends, old and new

The 1890s saw the strengthening of many old friendships and the growth of some new ones. In Malvern the Elgars' circle of friends included the Norbury sisters, Winifred and Florence (whose family estate adjoined Elgar's recently-acquired summer cottage, Birchwood), the architect Troyte Griffith, Alice's friends the Bakers and Dora Penny (Dorabella of the Enigma Variations), Lady Mary Lygon, Rosa Burley (a Malvern headmistress) and Dr George Sinclair, organist of Hereford Cathedral. One friendship which differed radically from the rest sprang from a professional association – that with August Johannes Jaeger, who had come to England from Düsseldorf and eventually taken a job as a production manager at the London music publishing house, Novello. Although employed at a relatively junior level, and not necessarily expected to exercise his musical judgement, Jaeger was quick to spot in Elgar's music the pointers to a new direction and sense of style which, coming from a continental tradition, he had found lacking in much of the music the firm already published. Jaeger recognized Elgar's talents and because of their close friendship was able to encourage him to greater musical heights than he might otherwise have attempted. Until Jaeger's death in 1909, the two men kept up a correspondence which reveals some of Elgar's most candid opinions and reflections on his music and his life.

By the end of the decade, Elgar had established a firm reputation as a composer of 'festival cantatas' and as such was increasingly in demand in the provinces. He was still depressed by the unappreciative attitude of Jaeger's superiors at Novello's. Although he was aware that his life in Malvern, particularly the time spent at the cottage at Birchwood, offered him the surroundings of country life which provided such a powerful stimulus to his creative spirit he still hoped for recognition further afield.

Fame, at last

In October 1898 Elgar wrote to Jaeger 'I have sketched a set of variations on an original theme: the variations have amused me because I've labelled 'em with the names of my particular friends . . .' This piece of music was the Enigma Variations. First performed on 19 June 1899 in London, the work at last brought Elgar the national acclaim he had so long yearned for.

The musical life of London, from bandstand to concert hall, attracted Elgar to moving there. However, although his Salut d'Amour *was performed at Crystal Palace (below) he had a generally unsuccessful time. After only one year he returned with Alice and his new daughter Carice (bottom), to Worcester.*

wrote many of his songs there, and it was through Schuster's fellow financier Edgar Speyer that Elgar met Richard Strauss who greatly admired Elgar's work. Another devoted friend, and wealthy patron of the arts, was Alfred Rodewald – a Liverpool textile magnate, who was also a talented conductor and double-bass player. His largely amateur Liverpool Orchestral Society achieved excellent standards and, in fact, later gave the first performance of the first two 'Pomp and Circumstance' marches, four days before they were played in London.

Lady Alice Stuart-Wortley, daughter of the Pre-Raphaelite painter Sir John Millais and the wife of Charles Stuart-Wortley, Conservative MP for a Sheffield constituency became a source of inspiration to Elgar and was a long-standing admirer of his

Thomas T. Patterson 'A Crowd Round a Bandstand' Fine Art Photographic Library

Sir James Guthrie 'Midsummer'. Royal Scottish Academy, Edinburgh/The Bridgeman Art Library

Elgar now stood on the threshold of a new chapter in his life. Along with his new-found fame came a number of new friends – friends who were to remain important to him for the rest of his life. Many of them were influential, either musically or financially, and belonged to the level of society to which Alice Elgar had been born. Accordingly, Alice encouraged her husband to move in 'society' circles as comfortably as she herself could. Elgar, however, sometimes found it hard to forget his own family background in 'trade', which, in the heavily stratified structure of Victorian and Edwardian society was considered respectable but socially inferior.

Among the new friends were the financier Frank Schuster, whose riverside home near Maidenhead, called 'The Hut', was a meeting place for musicians, painters and writers. His guests included Fauré, who

The Elgar Birthplace Trust

music. Their relationship was very close and there has been much speculation as to the extent of its intimacy. But it was essentially based on her response to his music and understanding of it – this naturally deepened to affection and provided him with an emotional creative impulse.

A second masterpiece

The turn of the century, then, saw a turn in Elgar's fortunes – even if he himself initially failed to see it ('All is flat, stale and unprofitable' – he wrote to Jaeger on 29 December 1899). One result of his improved circumstances was the move to a newly-built house (Craeg Lea) in Malvern Wells, where he began work on what was to become the oratorio – *The Dream of Gerontius*. Although he still continued some local teaching, he was now able to make more frequent visits to London, to concerts, opera, art exhibitions or simply to lunch at Pagani's restaurant or at his club.

The first performance of *The Dream of Gerontius,* in Birmingham in 1900, was, however, a disaster. The chorus-master died halfway through rehearsals, and the conductor, the great Hans Richter, had failed to appreciate the difficulties which Elgar's adventurous choral writing would present to a typically con-servative English choral society. Elgar was under-standably bitter that another masterpiece had not had a decent first hearing. Happily, the element of misfortune was short-lived. Attending the première in Birmingham with Jaeger was Julius Buths, musical director of the city of Düsseldorf and, despite the bad performance, he quickly recognized the true stature

Back in sight of the Malvern Hills Elgar spent his time teaching, composing and enjoying the companionship of a circle of close friends (below). When not composing or with friends Elgar could often be found experimenting in his laboratory 'The Ark' (bottom right).

of the work. When he returned to Germany he began work on a German translation and *The Dream of Gerontius* was duly performed in Düsseldorf in December 1901, and again at the Lower Rhine Festival in May the following year. The Elgars were fêted on both occasions – Richard Strauss proposed a toast 'to the welfare and success of the first English progressive composer'.

Back in England, Elgar scored much more immediate success with the *Cockaigne Overture* and the first two *Pomp and Circumstance Marches*. The trio of the first 'March' contained 'Land of Hope and Glory' – a tune the public took to with such fervour that it became almost a second national anthem. Elgar had captured the popular patriotic mood of the country in its Empire days. Meanwhile, Elgar returned to work on a sequence of three oratorios the idea for

which dated back to his school-days. The first, *The Apostles,* was completed for performance in Birmingham in October 1903. The concentrated effort put into its completion left Elgar exhausted; he was also troubled by eye-strain and throat infections. That winter the Elgars went to Italy where Elgar was at his most relaxed. As he had done on previous holidays he recorded his impressions musically, in the concert overture *In the South (Alassio),* which received its first performance at a three-day Elgar Festival held at Covent Garden in March 1904.

The year of acclaim

1904 was indeed a year of recognition and acclaim. Apart from the Festival at Covent Garden where he was recognized as a new force in English music there was the command to dine with the King, membership of a famous London club, the Athenaeum, and a Knight-hood. To Elgar, self-made and self-taught, these honours must have vindicated the snubs of his wife's family. The family moved to a larger house, Plas Gwyn, near Hereford, where modern amenities included a telephone, and in 1905 Elgar, who had always been wary of the prominent 'academic' musical establishment, was invited to join its ranks as first Professor of Music at Birmingham University taking a chair endowed by businessman, Richard Peyton.

In the same year honorary doctorates from Oxford and Yale were conferred upon him and he travelled to the United States to receive the Yale doctorate. He returned on three later occasions to conduct his music in the United States. It was wearing his Yale robes, shortly after his return, that he made his way through Worcester in a ceremony in which he was granted the freedom of the city. As he passed along the High Street he paused to bare his head in greeting to his father who, too frail to attend the celebrations, watched from his window above the family shop.

Back at Plas Gwyn, Elgar busied himself with the second part of the trilogy he had earlier begun with 'The Apostles'. The second part, *The Kingdom,* was ready for the Birmingham Festival of 1906. It was his last oratorio – although he began sketches for the third part, the trilogy remained incomplete. He turned instead to orchestral music and in the next five years completed two symphonies and the *Violin Concerto.*

for the death of Edward VII than with the jubilant spirit of coronation of the new King George V. Not only was there nothing of the patriotic fervour which the audience of the time expected but also the performance difficulties for the orchestra were great and it was some years before the Second Symphony took its rightful place in the orchestral repertoire.

Back to London

Elgar was disappointed by its lack of immediate success but there were other rewards — he was awarded the Order of Merit in Coronation Honours of 1911 and also acquired a permanent London home. By 1912 the family was installed in the imposing and palatial Severn House in Hampstead. It had a music-room, a billiard-room, a picture gallery and several acres of grounds.

Settled in London, the Elgars led a busy life, both professionally and socially. Lady Alice was in her

The Elgars continued to spend the winters in Italy. As always, the experience of being in a new place provided valuable creative stimulus, although it was usually only on his return to Plas Gwyn that Elgar would finally settle to the task of composing, transforming his musical sketches into their final form. At home he could also indulge in his favourite country pursuits, including bicycle rides and bird-watching, and he also revived an earlier interest in chemistry, turning one of the outbuildings into a laboratory called 'The Ark', where he amused himself with various experiments — on one occasion inadvertently blowing up a water barrel.

Unfitting as it might seem this was the milieu in which he composed what was acclaimed as his greatest work, his *First Symphony*. It received its first performance in 1908 — and in its first year was performed nearly 100 times in London, Vienna, Leipzig, St Petersburg, Sydney and the United States. At last the recognition which had eluded him in his early years as a composer now flowed in full measure.

Early in 1910 Elgar went to stay with the Schusters at 'The Hut' and here took up work on the *Violin Concerto*. Although himself doubtful of its quality, he was greatly encouraged, by his friends, the Stuart-Wortleys and the Speyers (Leonora Speyer was a professional violinist and played over parts of the new work for him).

Work on the concerto also resulted in a new friendship, with the violinist W. H. (Billy) Reed, later leader of the London Symphony Orchestra. Following a chance meeting in the street in London, Reed was invited back to Elgar's flat in New Cavendish Street to advise on bowings, fingerings and other technical aspects of the solo writing. Reed described how

on my arrival I found Sir Edward striding about with a number of loose pieces of manuscript which he was arranging in different parts of the room. Some were already pinned on the back of chairs, or fixed up on the mantelpiece ready for me to play . . .

It was the beginning of a firm friendship, which also became a professional association. By the time Elgar accepted an invitation from the London Symphony Orchestra to become its permanent conductor on Richter's retirement in 1911, Reed was its leader.

In May 1911 Elgar conducted his *Second Symphony* at its première in London. This symphony, reflective and elegiac in mood, was more in keeping with the previous year's national mood of mourning

element entertaining their many guests, and Sir Edward was busily engaged in conducting the London Symphony Orchestra as well as composing. In the capital city the Elgars were also able to indulge their love of the theatre. With the outbreak of war in 1914, however, Elgar's popularity rested in 'Land of Hope and Glory'. It was enormously popular but Elgar would have preferred that the sentiments expressed in the words provided by A. C. Benson were less swaggering. He himself worked hard both to sustain British music-making and at the same time to satisfy the public's appetite for suitable patriotic expression during the years of war. Apart from his commitment to the London Symphony Orchestra he also conducted the Hallé Orchestra in Manchester.

The war marked the decline of Elgar's popularity in Germany, not only for reasons of nationality, but also because many of the conductors and artists who had championed his early successes belonged to the

Elgar's friendship, in his later years, with the dramatist George Bernard Shaw (far left), renewed his interest in theatre, particularly after the death of his wife. In 1932 he met Yehudi Menuhin (right) then 16, who was the soloist for the 1932 recording of the Violin Concerto.

Elgar's life-long passion for the English countryside (below) and country pursuits, like cycling and walking, are reflected in the very 'Englishness' of his music.

generation now reaching old age and retirement. Elgar himself was approaching his sixties and, despite the outward successes of his wartime works – like *The Spirit of England* – he was neither happy nor in good health. Although he still gained pleasure from the company at Severn House, he began to long once again for the countryside. Alice Elgar, realizing her husband's need for peace and solitude, found a summer cottage, Brinkwells, near Fittleworth in Sussex. Elgar loved the new home which had a studio in the garden where he could work and was surrounded by woods in which he could walk for hours. Here he turned to chamber music, writing a string quartet, piano quintet and violin sonata. One other composition dates from the time at Brinkwells – the *Cello Concerto.* This was premièred in London in October 1919, and, as had happened before, in disgraceful circumstances. Part of the programme was conducted by Albert Coates, who overran his allotted rehearsal time by an hour. Elgar, greatest English composer of the day, who was to conduct his own work was not only kept waiting but also denied the opportunity of adequate rehearsal. The performance was consequently disastrous – as the critic Ernest Newman pointed out 'the orchestra made a lamentable public exhibition of itself'.

Swan-song

The *Cello Concerto* was in effect Elgar's swan-song. Although he lived for another fifteen years, he did not complete another major work.

The *Cello Concerto's* first performance was also the last witnessed by Lady Elgar, who died early in 1920. The effect of her death on her husband was shattering. For over thirty years it was she who had unfalteringly believed in him, who had supported and sheltered him, and seen the humble music-teacher she was disinherited for marrying, rise to become a national figure, sought-after by royalty, society and the British people.

Elgar survived Alice by 14 years but felt that his music vanished with her. He died on 23 February 1934 and is buried alongside her in the churchyard at St. Wulstan's, Little Malvern.

Enigma Variations Pomp and Circumstance

Enigma Variations *is a novel, intriguing series of musical character portraits of Elgar's friends, while the rousing* Pomp and Circumstance Marches *reflect the composer's spirit of patriotism.*

Enigma Variations

After a short and unhappy period in London, Elgar and his wife returned home to Malvern in 1891. Their family life settled into a comfortable pattern around the house (Forli) and Elgar embarked upon one of the most creative periods of his life, a decade full of new music that culminated in the *Variations on an Original Theme Op. 36* – the 'Enigma' Variations. This decade also saw the growth of many friendships. The 'friends who are pictured within' the variations were constantly on the scene, whether to play chamber music or golf, as holiday companions or as friends to go cycling or fox hunting with.

The idea for the *Variations* arose almost accidentally one October evening in 1898. It was shortly after the première of his cantata *Caractacus* at the Leeds Festival, and Elgar sat at the piano, almost idly toying with a fragment of melody. His wife Alice noticed the tune and asked him what it was. 'Nothing, but something might be made of it,' he replied. To amuse her, he started to play games with the tune, improvizing in a style that caricatured various people he knew. 'Powell would have done this', he said as he aped Powell's way of warming up at the keyboard – Hew Steuart-Powell was the pianist of the trio Elgar played with. Then the tune took on the noisy bluster of the trio's cellist Billy Baker. '. . . That is exactly the way WMB goes out of the room!', said Alice Elgar. Thoughtfully, she added, 'Surely you're doing something that has never been done before?'

It was a perceptive remark. Variation on a theme is as old as music itself, but to look at a theme through the character and characteristics of friends was a simple but wonderfully effective idea. Later that month, Elgar wrote to August Jaeger, his German friend and confident who worked for Elgar's publisher, Novello:

'. . . I have sketched a set of 'Variations' . . . on an original theme: the 'Variations' have amused me because I've labelled 'em with the nicknames of my particular friends – you are Nimrod. That is to say I've written the variations each one to represent the mood of the 'party' – I've liked to imagine the 'party' writing the var(-iation) him (or her) self and have

written what I think they wd. have written – if they were asses enough to compose. It's a quaint idea and the result is amusing to those behind the scenes & won't affect the hearer who 'nose nuffin'. What think you?'

He worked quickly. Friends were soon being teased with the piano sketches, and the orchestral score was ready in February 1899.

The Enigma

The première in London in June was a tremendous success and the piece soon acquired a lasting place in the hearts of English people. But Elgar's notes for the programme for the first performance started a mystery that has been puzzling the musical world ever since.

The enigma I will not explain – its 'dark saying' must be left unguessed, and I warn you that the apparent connection between the Variations and the Theme is often of the slightest texture; further, through and over the whole set another and larger theme 'goes', but is not played . . . . So the principal Theme never appears . . . the chief character is never on the stage.

In fact there are three mysteries if the initials that head each variation are

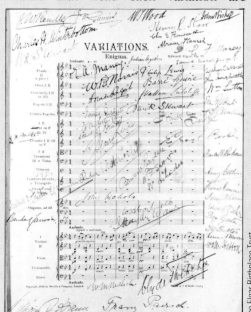

The 'Enigma Variations' seem to have sprung naturally and easily from Elgar's life in the Worcestershire countryside (right) and his relationships with his many friends.

The title page for the 'Enigma Variations', signed by the members of the orchestra who played the piece at the Leeds Festival in 1901 (left). Notice how the tiny copyright mark in the bottom lefthand corner belongs to Novello, the music publishing company that August Jaeger, Nimrod of the 'Variations', worked for.

included: this, at least, seems now at last to have been solved as the friends became identified. But this still leaves the twin mysteries of what Elgar called the 'dark saying which must be left unguessed' of the original theme, and the larger theme which 'goes' but is not played'.

The word 'Enigma' refers only to the theme, and it was added to the first page of music in pencil only after the orchestral score was completed. It is even possible that it was not Elgar who wrote the word. There has been some speculation on the inspiration for the word. It is known, for

instance, that when Elgar went to church a week before the score was completed, the First Letter of St Paul to the Corinthians, chapter 13, was read out (in Latin). This famous epistle, ends with the words 'For now we see through a glass darkly . . .' 'Darkly' is in Latin *aenigmate*.

The most satisfying suggestion is that the composer himself was the enigma and that the journey from the hesitant opening of the last variation charts his growing self-discovery as an artist, seen through the medium of his friends. This view is born out by Elgar's use of the *Enigma* theme in

The Music Makers, Op. 69, to represent the loneliness of the artist. He also sometimes signed himself with the theme's first four notes, and people have noticed the similarity of the rhythm of that short phrase to the natural speech rhythm of the words 'Edward Elgar'.

As for the 'larger theme', there are almost as many ideas as there are people to evolve them. Some people suggest for example, that the larger theme that links the *Variations* is, simply, friendship. Other people are more specific, and suggest that the Enigma theme is a counter-point to the

unheard, but ever-present, larger theme. Many believe that the mystery theme is actually a well-known tune and have devoted considerable effort to discovering which tune it is. T. van Houten, for instance, suggests *Rule, Brittannia!* and this is his reasoning. Like the *Variations,* the Enigma theme conceals someone's identity, which 'Dorabella' (of the tenth variation) as Elgar himself said, 'of all people should have guessed', because of her maiden name, Dora Penny; on the old penny coin is depicted Brittania, ruling the waves. Van Houten backs this up with a

The cosy domestic life (right) created by Elgar's wife Alice forms the basis of the first variation; in the second, Elgar mimicks the flamboyant piano style of his friend Hew Steuart-Powell (below); while the humorous gambolling of the oboe in the third sends up the ham acting of 'RBT' – Richard Baxter Townsend (bottom).

clever slant on Elgar's use of the word 'never' in his programme note, which he suggests may echo the words of the chorus of *Rule, Brittannia:* 'Britain never, never, never shall be slaves.' The suggestion is that Elgar took that 'never, never' segment of Arne's melody and used it as the opening four notes of his theme.

Van Houten's theory, published in the *Music Review* in 1976, concentrates on Elgar's patriotism. Another solution, which was published 50 years ago and took root in the composer's lifetime, focuses more on the theme of friendship. Richard Powell, the husband of 'Dorabella', suggested that the unheard theme was *Auld Lang Syne.* Dorabella was a close friend of Elgar's and

they had spent many happy hours together in the potting shed 'inventing new chemical combinations'. She confirmed her husband's theory 16 years later, saying that Elgar had told her, as well as other people, that the enigma was a secret melody that fitted his original theme as a counterpoint. This solution has been examined very closely, and the whole set — not just the theme — was carefully scrutinized by experts on the British Broadcasting Corporation's radio programme *Music Weekly,* who made a strong case for the *Auld Lang Syne* theory.

Another mystery surrounds 'Variations' –the identity of the person in the 13th. Some Elgar experts have suggested that it

secret, to avoid any damaging speculation. The conductor Leopold Stokowski recalled:

He was married; he was true to his wife, and yet he was in love with this girl. And this was a great tragedy in Elgar's life.

If Nicholas Reed's theory is correct, the thirteenth variation acquires a new and moving significance. The lady on the boat is Elgar's 'tender secret' leaving him to return to New York.

Elgar was plagued with requests to reveal all the secrets of the *Enigma Variations,* and to start with he enjoyed this game with people's curiosity. Yet some commentators have suggested that he became horribly embarrassed by what he had begun. He never actually denied that there were solutions, but whatever they were, he carried them to the grave, leaving behind a bewildering trail of clues, red herrings and tenuous associations.

Programme notes

From the subdued opening theme to the buoyant finale, the *Enigma Variations* show Elgar at his glorious best. The strict format he set himself produces music that is far more disciplined and controlled than some of his sprawling choral works of the same period. The *Variations* carry to a peak Elgar's genius for writing short, highly characterized vignettes.

The work opens with a clear but subdued statement of the theme which is to form the basis of all the subsequent variations:

The noisy, rumbustious 4th variation 'WMB' pictures the good-humoured bluster of William Meath Baker (below) as he announced the day's activities to his house guests. Richard Arnold (below right) is the subject of the reflective 5th variation.

Example 1
Andante

This theme hovers equivocally between minor and major keys, and the whole of the introductory section is shot through with uncertainty, as the composer sets out with trepidation on his voyage of self-discovery. Although the melancholy opening on strings gives way after a few bars to a rising, expansive figure introduced by solo clarinet, the tone is still yearning, and the music soon slides back to the anxious opening theme. Falling *sevenths* (a drop in pitch one note short of the full octave) punctuate the music almost like sighs.

Variation I (CAE)

CAE is Elgar's wife Alice, and the melody of the opening section here unfolds lovingly. Into the melody steals a graceful triplet figure on oboes and bassoons, apparently echoing the composer's habit of whistling to let his wife know when he came home. After settling into an evening calm, the variation suddenly erupts into a passionate outburst, with a roll upon the drums, before romantic horns lead to a quiet close.

Variation II (HDS-P) It was the idea of mimicking his friend Hew David Steuart-Powell's rather flamboyant piano style that was one of the inspirations for the *Variations.* First strings and then woodwind busily exchange rapidly cascading figures that suggest Steuart-Powell's taste for 'diabolic' scales. Then, with a little flourish, this brief, hectic variation leads into RBT.

Variation III (RBT) Richard Baxter Townsend was an amiable, reedy-voiced and rather eccentric actor who used to ride a tricycle, and this variation seems to capture his manner perfectly. Opening in the ponderous gait of the bassoon, it soon waddles into a series of delightful sliding runs in oboe and clarinet that caricature

had romantic significance for Elgar. Ernest Newman thought it might be Helen Weaver, the girl who finally rejected Elgar after an 18 month engagement. But, as Nicholas Reed points out, Helen Weaver was already dead at the time the *Variations* were composed, although she too had travelled overseas, to New Zealand. Reed puts forward a convincing case for a beautiful American lady named Julia 'Pippa' Worthington, who may also have been the inspiration for Elgar's Violin Concerto. There is some evidence to suggest that Elgar was deeply and passionately attached to Pippa for more than a decade and yet remained faithful to his wife Alice – hence the importance of keeping Pippa's identifty

Understanding music: 20th-century English music

'Das Land ohne Musik' – the land without music – was how Germans described Britain in the period between the death of Henry Purcell (1695) and Edward Elgar (born 1857). For 200 years Britain produced no native composer of equal stature to the many great composers born during the same time over the rest of Europe. Then, quite suddenly, Elgar appeared and re-established the reputation of English music. Thereafter it no longer seemed absurd to see the name of a British composer on a concert programme alongside names like Brahms or Beethoven.

During the 19th century, three seeds had been sown which were to bear fruit in the 20th century as the English musical renaissance. First, there was a revival of interest in English folk music (which reached a peak with the work of Cecil Sharp, who notated over 3000 tunes). Second, there was a similar revival of interest in the music of the Tudor madrigalists and the church music of William Byrd and Thomas Tallis. Third, the founding of the Royal College of Music in 1883 meant that music students in England could receive the kind of advanced training they previously had to seek abroad.

The next great composer that England produced was Frederick Delius (1862–1934). Born in Bradford of German parents, he lived in France from 1889 until his death. Although he wrote several operas and concertos, it will always be for his orchestral tone-poems that he will be best loved. Such works as *On Hearing the First Cuckoo in Spring* and *Summer Night on the River* perfectly suggest the mystical peace and inward rapture that the composer himself felt in contemplating nature. And nature, which played a large part in the inspiration of much of English music of the early 20th century, was just one of the features contributing to its distinct character.

Ralph Vaughan Williams (1872–1958) was, like his friend Gustav Holst, a student at the RCM and an enthusiast for older English music and folk-song collecting. In his *Fantasia on a Theme by Thomas Tallis* the string orchestra produces a quite deliberately archaic sound. In fact, Vaughan Williams frequently employs the older modes in place of modern scales, and this gives his music a haunting, even spititural quality, though his fourth symphony, on the other hand, is bitingly dissonant.

The voice of the later 1920s and 30s was that of William Walton (1902–83). His 'entertainment', *Facade* – a hybrid of Edith Sitwell's verses and Walton's tongue-in-cheek tunes – created a furore in 1923. Despite the power of the oratorio, *Belshazzar's Feast* and the Stravinskian rhythmic drive of his *First Symphony,* Walton is really a romantic with a modern mask. His concertos are lyrical, nostalgic and often, bittersweet.

Arnold Bax (1883–1953) wore no masks. Whether in his seven symphonies, his tone poems, or any of his numerous chamber works, he is in his own phrase, 'an unashamed romantic'. In 1942, he became Master of the King's Music, a post in which he was succeeded by Arthur Bliss (1891–1975). Best known for his music for the film, *Things to Come* (1935), Bliss's reputation would benefit from a revival of his stirring ballets, *Checkmate* (1937) and *Miracle in the Gorbals* (1944). Ballet was also significant in the output of Constant Lambert (1905–51), a pupil of Vaughan Williams at the RCM. But it is his *Rio Grande,* a setting of Sacherwell Sitwell's poem for piano, chorus and orchestra, which became his best loved piece with its synthesis of Delian nostalgia, jazz and

It was the energetic attempts of Arthur Troyte (right) to play the piano that inspired the 7th Variation, while Isabel Fitton (below) is mimicked in the 6th. Winifred Norbury's (below right) tinkling laugh is suggested in the 8th.

his faltering way of talking and walking.
Variation IV (WMB) William Meath Barker bursts noisily on to the scene as the entire orchestra bellows out the orders of the day to his house-guests in his blustering military style. A pause for breath has his guests smiling to themselves before WMB reads out the last instructions and leaves the room, banging the door behind him.
Variation V (RPA) Richard Arnold, son of the poet Matthew Arnold, is the subject of a more serious variation. It opens with a broad melody on strings, flowing serenely

South American rhythms.

The premiere of *Peter Grimes* in 1945 inaugurated the rebirth of English opera. The young composer, Benjamin Britten (1913–1976), went on to stake a claim as one of the greatest of all English musicians. His series of operas, song cycles, and choral works testify to his skill in writing for the voice and his ability to add to the poetry of words an intense musical poetry of his own.

Throughout the 1960s and 1970s the avant-garde was also represented in English music. Here, the composers of the Manchester School – Harrison Birtwhistle, Peter Maxwell Davies and Alexander Goehr – led the way.

From the start of his career, Sir Michael Tippett (born 1905) has shown a particular interest in the English musical tradition. As an opera composer, he has completed four major stage works and written his own highly symbolic librettos for each. The all-encompassing searching after truth of his recent magnum opus, *The Mask of Time* (1984) makes him the great seer among modern artists. In this work, the music is an expression, healthy and vital, of the contradictions within British people and society.

above the Enigma theme in the bass. Attractively contrasting woodwind interludes suggest the witty asides that punctuate his earnest conversation.

Variation VI (Ysobel) Isabel Fitton played the viola, and the opening bars of the gentle viola solo are a reminder of her difficulties at crossing between strings, as well as her calm beauty.

Variation VII (Troyte) Arthur Troyte Griffith was one of Elgar's closest friends, and his variation represents his impetuous, but hopelessly clumsy, attempts to play the piano under Elgar's instruction. The music is based on the middle section of the theme, and gathers in complexity as Elgar's vain attempts to impose some sense of order give way to the defiant close.

Variation VIII (WN) Winifred Norbury was one of the secretaries of the Worcestershire Philharmonic Society. The music really represents the beautiful 18th-century house where the Norbury family lived, but the graceful opening figure was inspired by her light way of laughing.

Variation IX (Nimrod) August Jaeger worked for Novello and was Elgar's closest musical confidant. He was German, and his surname means 'Hunter'; 'Nimrod' was the 'mighty hunter before the Lord' of the Bible. Elgar wrote: 'The variation . . . is the

Of the many friends who visited Elgar and passed many a happy hour with him in his beloved countryside (bottom), August Jaeger (below left) who was the subject of the beautiful Nimrod, and Dora 'Dorabella' Penny (below right) were among the closest.

The 11th variation pictures Dr Sinclair and his dog Dan (far left) as Dan struggles in the river.
The cello solo of the 12th variation was for Elgar's 'serious and devoted friend', the cellist Basil Nevinson (left).
Lady Mary Lygon (bottom left) was long assumed to be subject of the romantic 13th variation, but recent research suggests otherwise.

record of a long summer evening talk, when my friend discoursed eloquently on the slow movements of Beethoven . . . the opening bars are made to suggest the slow movement of Beethoven's eighth piano sonata (Pathetique).' This is the heart of the Variations; the first part of the theme is reworked into a broad melody of great nobility, in the warm key of E flat. 'I have omitted your outside manners and have only seen the good lovable honest SOUL in the middle of you.'

Variation X (Dorabella) Dora Penny's variation is subtitled 'Intermezzo', and its lightly scored texture is made up of three elements: a trilling strings figure, with its woodwind answer (suggested by her slight stammer) and an affectionate viola solo, derived from the middle part of the theme.

Variation XI (GRS) Dr G. R. Sinclair was organist at Hereford Cathedral and had a bulldog called Dan. As Sinclair and Elgar were walking along the River Wye once, Dan fell down the bank into the river, and had to paddle upstream before he could climb out, whereupon he let out a rejoicing bark. 'Set that to music', challenged Sinclair;

the results are the opening five bars. The music is based on a hugely energetic transformation of the theme's middle section, and the light staccato passages in the bass, while representing Dan's furious paddling, are also a deferential nod to Sinclair's impeccable pedal technique on the organ.

Variation XII (BGN) Basil Nevinson was the cellist in a piano trio with Elgar and Steuart-Powell, and the cello solo depicts Elgar's attachment to this 'serious and devoted friend' in music every bit as expressive as Nimrod.

Variation XIII (***) Elgar wrote of this variation that, 'the asterisks take the place of the name of a lady who was, at the time of the composition, on a sea voyage'. The drums suggest the distant throb of the engines of a liner over which the clarinet quotes a phrase from Mendelssohn's *Calm Sea and Prosperous Voyage*.

The Mendelssohn quotation is heard twice followed by a powerfully evocative passage swelling in a majestic crescendo as the great liner draws nearer, and subsiding as she slips into the distance.

Variation XIV (EDU) This is Elgar himself, with the nickname Edu coined by his wife. The buoyant, assured opening sets the mood of music intended as a retort to those of his friends who were 'dubious and generally discouraging' about his future as a composer. We hear again his wife's music, and Nimrod is woven into the great finale.

Pomp and Circumstance Marches

Whatever Elgar's difficulties and uncertainties, his public front was that of an English gentleman. He fervently believed in his country and his support of social traditions was wholehearted. He was proud that his music could express so succinctly patriotic sentiments.

The phrase 'pomp and circumstance' is actually a quote from Shakespeare's play *Othello*. The full phrase is, 'O farewell . . . all quality, Pride, pomp and circumstance of glorious war!' It occurs in a speech

Elgar was a great believer in the kind of pageant created to celebrate Queen Victoria's Diamond Jubilee in 1897 (above), and the 'Pomp and Circumstance' marches are his tribute to England's heritage of pageantry.

where Othello is renouncing the 'counterfeit clamour' of war and it is possible that Elgar too was actually sending up the false heroics of militarism. If so, such an interpretation was lost on the public.

When the first two marches were premièred at one of the Henry Wood Promenade Concerts at Queens Hall, London, in 1901, the audience response was overwhelming. 'I shall never forget the scene at the close of the first of them, the one in A major,' wrote Henry Wood later, 'The people simply rose and yelled. I had to play it again – with the same result; in fact, they refused to let me go on with the programme . . . Merely to restore order, I played the march a third time.' The middle tune of the march was, as Elgar had predicted, 'a tune that will knock 'em – knock 'em flat'. King Edward VII loved it and suggested it be given words and incorporated into his Coronation Ode, planned for his coronation in 1902, although this was delayed because of his sudden appendicitis. The big tune from the first march was transformed into a magnificent finale for the *Coronation Ode*,

with the aid of some suitably stirring words written by A. V. Benson. As *Land of Hope and Glory,* the tune swept through England and all but replaced *God Save the Queen* as the national anthem. It reached the height of its popularity at the outbreak of World War I. On the night of August 4, 1914 *Land of Hope and Glory* was sung defiantly in pubs, bars and clubs throughout London.

Programme notes

The first march in D major opens with a brief curtain-raiser in the key of E flat, before strutting off with breezy self-confidence into the march proper. But it is in the middle section, the *trio,* that the march really gets going, for this section is based on the famous tune of *Land of Hope and Glory.*

The second, in A minor, has an attractive trio, with its woodwind scoring reminiscent of a dance by Dvořák. The third is in the dark key of C minor, with a delicately scored trio that develops into a broad, sonorous melody. The fourth, in G major, is nearly as well known as the first and was used as the wedding march for the Prince and Princess of Wales in 1980; the lovely middle section has the characteristic Elgarian marking *Nobilmente* (to be played nobly). The fifth, written in 1930, starts with a lightly bouncing C major *vivace,* easing to the heartfelt yearning of the middle section.

Great interpreters

Clarion

FURTHER LISTENING

Falstaff
Elgar had a deep love for Shakespeare, and this symphonic study faithfully and imaginatively depicts one of the Bard's great comic characters in music. It is a full-blooded picture; swaggering and heavy, while Elgar's music for Henry V is a closely-observed combination of dignity and splendour. The interacting themes supply their own story, paralleling the gradual disintegration of a friendship as the fun-loving Prince becomes the serious King.

Symphony No 1
Elgar's two symphonies have only in recent years begun to establish a truly international reputation, and the reason for this slow acceptance has often been given as their 'Englishness.' But the music, with its glorious, rich colours and closely-worked themes is much closer to the great central-European tradition of Beethoven and Brahms. The First Symphony is a triumphant demonstration of the composer's mastery of symphonic form, and is a moving work.

Violin Concerto
This concerto is a beautifully-balanced work in every way: in the relationship between soloist and orchestra, in the balance of light and shade in the music, and in the expression of deeply felt emotion. Elgar's full mastery of orchestral colours and sonorities is amply demonstrated, as is his complete empathy with the violin, both in the solo and in the orchestral roles.

Norman Del Mar (conductor)
Del Mar studied under Vaughan Williams and Constant Lambert at the Royal College of Music. He progressed rapidly as a horn player and, in 1946, was hired in that capacity by the Royal Philharmonic. In this period he also founded and conducted the Chelsea Symphony Orchestra. Recognizing his talent, Beecham engaged him in 1947 as the RPO's musical assistant. He continued his rise in English music circles becoming Assistant Conductor at Sadlers Wells Opera in 1948, and Principal Conductor with the English Opera Group the following year. During the 1950s he was associated with the Yorkshire Symphony Orchestra, and became a Professor of Conducting at the Guildhall School of Music. In 1960 he started a term as conductor of the British Broadcasting Corporation's Scottish Orchestra, before going to Goteborg as Chief Conductor of their Symphony Orchestra. His long association with the British Broadcasting Corporation Orchestra, which later became the Academy of the BBC, was started in 1966 and in 1974 he was named Principal Conductor.

During the 1970s, he also became more active as a freelance conductor, particularly in Scandinavia. A composer in his own right, Del Mar has made many fine recordings, and was made a Commander of the British Empire in 1975.

IN THE BACKGROUND
'Jewel in the crown'

Throughout Elgar's lifetime Britain was at the peak of her imperial power and ruled colonies the world over. And it was India, in the days of the Raj, that was 'the jewel in the imperial crown'.

British rule in India grew out of the British East India Company's commercial interests there in the 18th century. And, as the painting **The East offering its riches to Brittania** *(above) shows, India certainly had much to give. But by the mid-19th century simple trading involvement had grown into the belief that Britain had a 'sacred duty' to oversee the nation – by force, if necessary.*

Exotic goods (left), native craftsmanship and low labour costs made India a profitable marketplace for Britain.

At the stroke of midnight on 14 August 1947, British rule in India (The Raj) came to an end. For just under two centuries the huge subcontinent had been 'the brightest jewel in the royal crown', and far more than the countless other British colonies dotted around the world, it had been the very symbol of the British Empire.

British ascendancy in India fell into two chapters of nearly equal length. For the first century, British India was simply a commercial empire established and run by the East India Company. Known colloquially as 'John Company', it exercised control over three-fifths of the subcontinent by the fateful year of 1857. Then, seemingly out of the blue, came the greatest trauma of the Victorian era – the Indian Mutiny. The savagery of the Mutiny and the brutality of its suppression left permanent scars – on the British, who never again felt they could trust the Indians among whom they lived, and on the Indians, who were left in no doubt that the 'natural' authority of the British Empire, in the final analysis, rested on force.

From the ashes of the Mutiny emerged modern India – that is to say, the India that existed, more or less unchanged, until the end of British rule. On 1 November 1858, the responsibility for administering the subcontinent passed from the East India Company to the British Crown – in effect, the British Government acting through an appointed Viceroy, an Indian Civil Service and an overhauled Indian Army.

When, on New Year's Day 1877, Queen Victoria was proclaimed Empress of India, the imperial edifice was now complete. The Raj was now an established fact of life – if one of the most improbable facts ever. From a small island off the west coast of Europe – Britain – something like 5000 officials administered for generations a vast area 6000 miles distant that teemed with 300 million people – then about one-fifth of the world's population. They did this, moreover, against a geographical landscape harshly unfamiliar, in a climate as unhealthy as it was uncomfortable, and in the midst of such varied races and cultures that to gain more than a passing knowledge of them would require the study of a lifetime. Above all, they did it free from self-doubt, secure in the belief that theirs was a noble duty.

Victorian notions of such a duty look suspiciously hypocritical to modern eyes. But not so very long ago, a great many people considered the British Empire to be almost divine in its foundation, and as likely to lead, through righteous administration, to the relief of the miseries and evils of the world. British rule in India was, therefore, considered a sacred trust, and one which would confer immense benefits on India itself. George Nathaniel Curzon, one of the ablest and most dedicated Viceroys (1899–1905) wrote without a trace of irony,

*The sacredness of India haunts me like a passion.
To me the message is carved in granite, hewn in the rock of doom: that our work is righteous and that it shall endure.*

The social pyramid
The Viceroy stood at the pinnacle of the Anglo-Indian structure – a social structure far more tightly regimented than anything to be found in contemporary Victorian England. In fact, it has often been remarked that the social order of the Raj bore a marked resemblance to the Hindu caste system. Senior civil servants and administrators cor-

The British wrought radical social changes in India, such as the abolition of 'Suttee' – the burning of widows on their husbands' funeral pyres (a rite depicted with Victorian delicacy, below). Such practices reinforced the belief that Britain was 'obliged' to tame and civilize the country.

responded to the priestly class of Brahmins, and enjoyed special authority and privileges befitting their lofty status. Then came the military officers of both the British and Indian Army, equivalent to the Hindu warrior caste. Next came businessmen, plantation owners and others of middle class, corresponding to the low-caste Hindu merchants. Finally, the equivalents of the Hindu outcasts were the British Tommy and, still lower, the half-caste Eurasian.

Everyone knew precisely where he stood in the social order. He could find out where anyone else stood, too, by simply looking at the relevant Civil or Military Lists. The *India Office List* for 1899 comprised 700 pages of minute type, setting out the title, duties and salary of every British official in India, from haughtiest judge to humblest clerk.

This social pyramid had an effect on the behaviour of both British and Indians. The first thing a young man learned when he arrived was that he must conform to his status. In addition, he was a member of the ruling race, and he was to behave as such. This meant, above all, that his relations with native Indians were to be conducted along rigorously formal lines. The gravest sin possible was to 'go native': the penalty, ostracism from the British community.

Fraternization was a theme much explored by Rudyard Kipling. Kipling was widely read, and so served to reinforce the taboo. In a preface to an unpleasant little parable entitled 'Beyond the Pale', he asserts,

A white man should, whatever happens, keep to his own caste, race and breed. Let the White go to the White and the Black to the Black. Then whatever trouble falls is in the ordinary course of things neither sudden, alien, nor unexpected. This is the

Until the Indian Mutiny of 1857, British army officers had no idea that Indian soldiers were capable of disloyalty. Side by side, British and Indian troops had fought together in countless battles (above), clearing India's borders of invading bands of brigands.

story of a man who wilfully stepped beyond the safe limits of decent everyday society, and paid for it heavily . . . He took too deep an interest in native life; but he will never do so again.

This cautionary tale speaks volumes about the insecurities that haunted the British in India. They abhorred the idea of integration. They were not settlers, much less immigrants. They came to India to do a job, and if they survived long enough, they went home to England in their retirement.

This estrangement of rulers from the ruled resulted, at best, in a high-minded paternalism on the part of the British official. He attempted to preserve public order, promote private justice, stamp out barbaric practices such as suttee (Hindu widows burning themselves to death on their husband's funeral pyres) and alleviating the effects of natural disasters such as famine. At worst, it led to a demoralizing hypocrisy. As one disenchanted Englishman put it in a letter back home: *'The English contempt proceeds in the main from English ignorance, and English ignorance is accompanied, as so often happens, by English bluster.'*

Whether approached in a spirit of altruism or disdain, the task of uplifting the Indian masses to any extent was probably hopeless. The population was huge, the annual rainfall upon which its harvests relied was unreliable. Famine stalked the land. Between 1876 and 1878, for example, successive failures of the monsoon exposed some 36 million people to famine. Five million died. The famine of 1896-7 brought 62 million to the edge of starvation and again claimed about 5 million lives.

If famine was an ever-present threat, poverty and disease were ever-present realities. English sensibilities recoiled from conditions that condemned millions upon millions to mercifully short lives of squalor. In a Sanitary Survey made in 1896, the house drains in Calcutta were described as follows:

In a large number of cases, the downpipe was broken 5–15ft from the ground, and the water,

The responsibility for governing and implementing British policy in India was invested in the Viceroy. One of the ablest and most dedicated – and the youngest – Viceroys was Lord Curzon (left), Viceroy between 1899-1905.

The Great Durbars were spectacular gatherings of British and Indian notables. These events were, essentially, public relations exercises organized to promote British prestige. The first Great Durbar was in 1876 when Queen Victoria was declared Empress of India (below).

urine and liquid sewage from the houses was simply splashing on the ground, fouling the whole gali (lane), and soaking the walls of the houses . . . Many of the interiors of the dwelling were pitch dark even in broad daylight; the rats ran about fearlessly as if it were the middle of the night. Walls and floors alike are damp with contamination from liquid sewage which is rotting, and for which there is no escape.

A crowded community awash in sewage: perfect conditions for cholera, and the stinking slums of Calcutta duly won the title 'world headquarters of cholera'. In India as a whole, 800,000 died of the disease in 1900 alone. Malaria and tuberculosis killed far more. And normally non-fatal afflictions like dysentery and diarrhoea took a dreadful toll. Plague, spread by rats, was endemic. In the quarter-century beginning 1896, it claimed 34 million victims.

Surviving these mass killers was no guarantee of health. At any given time, there were probably a million lepers and half that number blinded by infectious eye disease. An estimated 5 per cent of the adult population endured the ravages of venereal disease. Children readily fell prey to whooping cough, diptheria, meningitis and anything else that could grip a physique weakened by malnutrition and mired in filth. There was a desperate shortage of doctors, nurses and medical facilities.

The British in India were not indifferent to the plight of India's masses. They built thousands of miles of railway, which not only improved communication in general, but also made it possible for food to be transported more quickly from areas of plenty to those stricken by drought. Irrigation schemes, too, were undertaken as a means of improving yield and reducing poverty. In 1901 Lord Curzon appointed an Irrigation Commission, which

put forward a 20-year programme of development. By the end of that period more than 10 per cent of the total area of British India under cultivation – 20 million acres – was served by irrigation.

The scale of India's problems, however, would have defeated the most determined and sweeping efforts at social and economic reform, even if such reforms had been the purpose of the Raj. They were not. An article in the *Asiatic Review* for 1889 swept aside any such pretensions:

Let us have the courage to repudiate the pretence, which foreigners laugh at and which hardly deceives ourselves, that we keep India only for the

benefit of their country and in order to train them for self-government. We keep it for the sake of the interests and the honour of England . . .

The great Durbars

The honour, more, the glory of imperial England reached its apogee in the great Durbars of the Raj. The Durbar was an old Mogul custom of holding court, and the British readily adapted it to their own needs. Normally, Durbars were simply made up of petitioners gathering outside an official's home or office each morning. At a more exalted level they were the various official gatherings held at the court of the Viceroy in the course of the year. On three occasions, however – in 1876, 1903 and 1911 – truly magnificent Durbars were staged outside Delhi.

The first of these great Durbars was to celebrate the proclamation of Queen Victoria as Empress of India. The second, to mark the coronation of Edward VII, was the ceremonial high point of Lord Curzon's tenure. In terms of scale and grandeur it far surpassed the coronation celebrations in London. Curzon and

The ordinary Indian lived in atrocious conditions of poverty and squalor (above left), yet the regional rajas and princes (above) were vastly wealthy. Indeed, it was from the latter that Queen Victoria received some of her richest tributes.

A tea planter, his wife and neighbours sit out (below) beyond the 'verandah' of their 'bungalow' (both words were added to the language during the Raj). Life for these ex-patriots was a mixture of adventure, formal socializing, and boredom.

his staff made their grand entrance on elephants, to take the salute in a march-past of 40,000 men of the Indian Army and the British Army in India. Scores of princes and maharajahs, bedecked with the most fabulous garments and jewels, came to pay homage to the King-Emperor, as represented by the Viceroy. And in a revealing touch Curzon banned the hymn *Onward Christian Soldiers* from the religious service because of its seditious sentiments:

Thrones and crowns may perish,
Kingdoms rise and wane . . .

The third great Durbar, in 1911, even outshone Curzon's. It marked the accession of George V, and the King-Emperor and Queen Mary made the voyage from England for the occasion. An army of 20,000 workers prepared the site for the Durbar, and a fortune was spent building drains and polo grounds for 233 camps extending over 25 square miles. The

From the British point of view the Indian soldiers' virtues of loyalty and heroism drew a great respect, as the Victorian music hall song (title page, right), shows.

The British Army in India was made up of both Indians and British – usually Indian soldiers under British command (below right). This system could not have worked without a certain willingness of the native troops to submit to foreign domination.

This Song may be Sung in public without fee or Licence, except at Theatres and Music Halls.

HOW · INDIA · KEPT · HER · WORD.

Written by
J. P. HARRINGTON,

Composed by
GEORGE LE BRUNN,

CHORUS.
India's Reply in the days gone by,
To other nations may have been absurd,
But when Britain's flag unfurl'd, They prov'd to all the world,
How the Sons of India kept their word.
SUNG BY

LEO · DRYDEN.

The British soldier though he might work out his entire career in India, could never be more than an onlooker of Indian society (above). Due to the rigid rules of the social system, to mix with the natives was to risk being outcast by his fellow men.

royal camp alone spread across 85 acres, with green lawns, red roads, and roses from England.

The everyday life of a minor official

For the most part, life in the Raj was humdrum. A typical official would be posted to a remote up-country station, at least for the first few years of his service. If he was lucky, he would find himself in a favoured province such as Punjab or the United Provinces. If not, it might be the steamy jungles of Upper Burma, or the parched Sind Desert. The station itself would be broken down into self-contained communities – the native quarter on the 'wrong' side of the railway tracks, the British on the other, complete with church, offices, public buildings, and perhaps a public garden. Invariably, the station club and the best bungalows reserved for

senior officials were at the centre, giving way towards the perimeter to lesser bungalows, police and military garrisons.

A typical bungalow was surrounded by a verandah; the rooms inside were spacious. At the rear, separate from the bungalow, stood the kitchen, with the servants' quarters nearby. There was no servant problem. A book describing Anglo-Indian Life, published in 1878, suggests 27 servants as appropriate for a reasonably affluent family in Calcutta, 14 as sufficient for a bachelor. Children, and sometimes even the family dog, had their own servant.

The first step a new arrival took, on reaching the station, was to don formal clothes and present his card at the door of senior officials. After an appropriate interval this would elicit a dinner invitation. He would also apply at once for membership of the station club.

In preparation for the day's work, he would rise early, taking tea and toast before six. This would allow a period of exercise – riding, in all likelihood – during the relative cool of the morning. Breakfast would be at nine, then the day's work began.

It was probably tedious. He was a tiny part of the largest bureaucracy in the world, and everything that bureaucratic machine did was committed to paper. Huge piles of written memoranda and minutes were carried by a horde of messengers from office to office across the land. Officials spent most of their working hours reading and writing, and, in consequence, it took an eternity to accomplish the most trivial task.

The working day ended at five, with dinner at seven followed by cards or billiards or reading. The dinner might be a dinner party; there might be a chukka of polo in the early evening. But the overwhelming pattern was one of deadly monotony. There was a great deal of heavy drinking.

The one perquisite was The Tour, which was encouraged by most branches of the service. Freed from the boredom and red tape of the office, the *sahib* (gentleman) would set out to inspect his territory. It might be a huge area requiring weeks of

touring. Sleeping under canvas by night, enjoying the hospitality and deference accorded a VIP by day, it was the perfect way to savour the delights of India during the 'Cold Weather' – that is to say, the winter.

The young official on his first tour was certain to be a bachelor: it was frequently stipulated in his contract that he remain one for a certain period of time, or until he reached a certain status. During the 'Hot Weather' he would be unlikely, in any case, to encounter any unmarried young women, because they would have been packed off to the more temperate hills. When the Cold Weather came (mid-October) the situation changed overnight, just as summer clothing gave way to winter clothing regardless of the weather. For the next four months it was a whirl of dances: tea-dances and club-dances, dinner-dances and the Viceroy's Annual Ball.

If the young official failed to find himself a wife during the hectic match-making of the Cold Weather, he could always return to England to seek one (where the competition was less stiff), at the end of his first tour of duty. Such a tour of duty was usually an unbroken period of four or five years.

For his English bride, the sea voyage to India would be the beginning of an adventure for which she could not possibly be prepared. After the opening of the Suez Canal in 1869, the journey was reduced to four weeks from anything up to six months by the Cape route. It was a luxury cruise aboard one of the great ocean-going liners. But on disembarking at the gateway of India in Bombay, a new life began. She was now a *memsahib* (gentleman's lady).

She would live in a rented house with rented furniture, changing both maybe every year, without any say in the matter. All day long she was alone in the house with a clutch of servants who could understand her no better than she could understand them, and shared her unwillingness to break down the barriers to communication. If she was married to

an army officer, she might be on her own for months while he was away on active service. When she had children, she could expect to nurse them through a host of illnesses and, assuming they survived to reach school age, send them away to England.

Such a bleak picture does not, of course, describe the Indian years of every young woman who made the voyage to Bombay. Many refused to succumb to the climate, or to the equally energy-sapping routine of a typical household. Many accompanied their husbands on tour, living in tents and eating whatever local concoctions were placed before them. Many, in the later years of the Raj, openly showed an interest in Indian society, concerned themselves in the welfare of their servants and the wider India beyond their own doorstep. Many seldom thought of England.

The end, when it came, was sudden, though nationalistic movements had existed for a hundred years. Ironically, a concerted struggle for independence only became possible because of the achievement of the Raj. Improved lines of communications meant that sympathetic political groups could communicate and unite. The use of English throughout the country meant that political debate could take place between intellectual Indians from whatever region. It also exposed the educated to the works of Western liberals who questioned imperialism and recommended democracy. Englishmen who could so fervently colonize foreign soil in the interests of their own flag taught Indians to think in nationalistic terms themselves. Once India had realized the possiblity of saying 'No' to British domination, there was no way that domination could profitably continue.

As the last Viceroy (Queen Victoria's great-grandson, Lord Louis Mountbatten) prepared to sign over the Raj, the British packed their bags for the last voyage home. Their fairest epitaph has been provided by the historian who wrote: 'By and large, they meant well.'

The legacy of the Raj included a railway network on a scale to match the vast size of the country. The huge Victoria Rail Terminus, Bombay (above), built in a mixture of Victorian and Indian styles, reflects the scale of British involvement in India.

THE GREAT COMPOSERS

Richard Strauss

1864–1949

Richard Strauss was hailed as both the last of the great Romantics and as the composer of the 'music of the future.' He was also renowned as an intuitive conductor, especially gifted in interpreting the works of Wagner and Mozart. In his operas, songs and instrumental works, Strauss wrote in an expressive, complex style, showing a superb mastery of orchestral resources. Strauss was a public man, his reputation open to much controversy; today, however, he is acknowledged as a master of his time. Among his many fine orchestral pieces the epic tone poems Also Sprach Zarathustra and Till Eulenspiegel, both analysed in the Listener's Guide, *stand out as striking symphonic works. In the period when Strauss wrote most of his mighty tone poems, an event occurred that was to have consequences for the world – the birth of Adolf Hitler, whose rise to power is chronicled in* In The Background.

Richard Strauss was an uncommonly gifted young man, and his family's love of music and comfortable financial position in Munich gave him the security to develop his gifts. Before he was twenty, he had published several works and made his conducting debut. Soon, he was at the peak of both his careers: as a conductor he was in great demand, accepting the chief post with the famed Royal Court Opera in Berlin, and as a composer, he had achieved much acclaim for his tone poems and his one-act operas. His personal life attracted almost as much attention as his extraordinary works – dramatic public rows with his wife, the singer Pauline de Ahnas, accusations of greediness, and charges of impartiality in his new post as co-director of the Vienna State Opera. His association with Nazi Germany also tarnished his name, although as an artist he genuinely felt himself beyond politics. But the brilliant compositions of his final years did much to encourage a positive re-assessment of his remarkable career.

'Music of the future'

A phlegmatic, dour-looking man, Richard Strauss was the last of the great Romantic composers. A true master of the orchestra, his spectacular compositions have ensured him lasting popularity.

Richard Strauss is one of the more enigmatic figures of 20th century music. An outwardly conservative, worldy man who sometimes seemed to take almost as much interest in making money as making music, he created a series of stunning, sensational compositions that made him one of the most-talked about men of his time. Newspapers were full of him and his music – and if they could not write about him, they would write about his dominating wife Pauline. For more than 20 years, a stream of brilliant, evermore impressive pieces flowed from his pen to thrill the world – symphonic poems such as *Till Eulenspiegel* and *Also sprach Zarathustra* and operas such as *Salome* and *Elektra*. He was hailed as both the natural successor to Liszt and Wagner and the writer of 'the music of the future'.

Then, around the time of World War 1, his inspiration, many music critics felt, seemed to evaporate and his compositions appeared simply to repeat old formulas. Stravinsky came to write of one of Strauss's later works 'bombast and rodomontade . . . treacly . . . the music chokes me'. His reputation became further tarnished by his association with Nazism in the 1930s. Only now are critics beginning to re-appraise his later music and discover some of the magical elements that made his earlier works amongst the most popular of all compositions of the last hundred years.

The young lion

Richard Strauss was certainly born in the kind of circumstances that would allow his talent to flourish. His family was comfortably off, for his father's second wife Josephine Pschorr (Strauss's mother) brought to the marriage a substantial share of her family's brewing fortune. More importantly, Strauss's father Franz was a brilliant hornplayer, a principal in the Munich Court Orchestra. Franz Strauss was famous for his beautiful playing of Wagner's music, which was strange for he was very conservative in his tastes and detested Wagner's music – he was often involved in bitter rows with Wagner and Wagner's friend and champion, the conductor Hans von Bülow. The Strauss household was always full of music, for Franz also ran an amateur orchestra known as 'Wilde Gung'l' which would often rehearse in the house. It was through the Wilde Gung'l that the young composer heard his earliest compositions

Richard Strauss (right) aged 39, photographed while attending the London Strauss Festival in 1903. Though by this time he had composed his great tone poems he was later to achieve still greater fame and recognition.

36

Bildarchiv Preussischer Kulturbesitz

weeks, however, Bülow resigned, following a quarrel with Brahms over the latter's new *Fourth Symphony,* and Strauss found himself in charge. The Duke proposed cuts in the orchestral establishment and, although Strauss was offered an extension of his contract, he opted instead to return to Munich as third conductor there.

But his brief stay in Meiningen had brought a friendship that was to influence profoundly the course of his musical development. His new friend was Alexander Ritter, a violinist who knew Liszt and Wagner well and had married Wagner's niece. By deepening Strauss's knowlege of Liszt's and Wagner's music (an area of his musical education omitted by his father), Ritter provided Strauss with a new and original artistic direction.

New ideas must search for new forms – this basic principle of Liszt's symphonic works, in which the

Richard Strauss was the first child of Josephine Pschorr (above) and Franz Josef Strauss (above right). Encouraged by his father, who was the principal born player of the Munich Court Orchestra, Richard began music lessons at the tender age of four.

played properly – undoubtedly contributing to his later mastery of the orchestra.

Richard was born on 11 June 1864 and began taking piano lessons at the age of four. He showed a prodigious talent and was composing small pieces by the time he was six. There is nothing very exciting about these works, nor indeed about any of his early compositions, for his father's influence was thoroughly traditional. Nevertheless, many of the works written in his teens were highly competent, and as he approached the time to go to University in 1882, they were being performed more and more. His *Symphony in D minor,* for instance, was played by the Munich Court Orchestra under its celebrated conductor Hermann Levi in 1880. Naturally, a musical career beckoned and although he did go to the University of Munich in 1882, to study philosophy, aesthetics and the history of art, he remained there only two terms.

In the following winter (1883–4) Richard made his first trip to Berlin. Here he went to the opera, developed a lifelong passion for playing cards and made many friends. But the most significant event of the trip was his meeting with Hans von Bülow. When Bülow saw a copy of Strauss's *Serenade* for 13 wind instruments, he was impressed and, despite the disagreements with Strauss's father, generously described Strauss as 'An uncommonly gifted young man – by far the most striking personality since Brahms'.

Bülow immediately commissioned Strauss to write another piece, the *Suite,* also for 13 instruments and arranged for it to be premièred when the orchestra visited Strauss's home town of Munich. He even invited Strauss himself to conduct the performance. The young composer was delighted and, explaining his lack of conducting experience, asked when the rehearsal would be, Bülow replied that the orchestra did not have time to rehearse on tour! But Strauss's début as a conductor was a great success.

Soon, Strauss's talents on the rostrum became so obvious that, the following autumn, von Bülow appointed him as his assistant at Meiningen. Here he began his apprenticeship in earnest. Within a few

poetic idea was really the formative element, became henceforward the guiding principle for my own symphonic work!

Touring

Back in Munich, however, Strauss found himself entrusted only with works then considered third-rate. He compensated by an increasing amount of guest conducting visiting Frankfurt, Hamburg, Cologne, and Leipzig, where he 'made a new and very attractive acquaintance in Herr Mahler, who seemed to me a highly intelligent musician and conductor – one of the few modern conductors who know about tempo rubato' (conducting with a certain amount of give-and-take, with regard to tempo). The acquaintance was to develop into a long friendship during which Strauss was quick to champion Mahler's music.

Perhaps the most important trip in Strauss's life at

In the winter of 1883–4 Strauss left Munich University and made his first visit to Berlin where he immersed himself in the artistic and musical life of the city, frequenting both opera house and café (below). Here, he met the famous conductor and composer Hans von Bülow (right). Von Bülow was greatly impressed by Strauss's work and described him as 'by far the most striking personality since Brahms'.

this time, however, was a holiday he took in August 1887 in his mother's family villa in Feldating, where he made the acquaintance of a neighbouring family, the de Ahnas. The eldest daughter, Pauline, at 25 two years older than Strauss, had studied singing in Munich but had so far failed to establish a professional career. Strauss recognized her potential as a singer and, at the same time, fell deeply in love. He also resolved to promote Pauline's singing career and, when he obtained the post of assistant conductor in Weimar in October 1889, he took Pauline with him.

Life in Weimar began promisingly enough with the first performance of *Don Juan* there in November 1889. It was his greatest success to date and established him at the forefront of the younger generation of German composers. This was a time of intense creative activity for Strauss and he had soon completed his first opera, *Guntram*.

However, getting *Guntram* staged was much harder than Strauss anticipated because of the excessive demands made on the voices of the principal characters. Eventually he decided to perform the work with Pauline and another of his pupils, the tenor Heinrich Zeller, in the leading roles.

Zeller found the score taxing and in one rehearsal was made to go back over several passages. Pauline, on the other hand, knew her role well and sang on uninterrupted. Finally she stopped and turned to Strauss complaining 'Why don't you interrupt me?' 'Because you know your part!' he replied. But Pauline was not prepared to lose her share of the attention and with the words 'I *want* to be interrupted!' threw her score at him and ran to the dressing room with Strauss trailing behind. It seemed to the orchestra that a violent argument was going on between composer and singer in the dressing room. When Strauss emerged half an hour later, he was told that the players were shocked by Pauline's behaviour and refused to play in any opera in which she sang. Strauss replied 'That pains me very much, for I have just become engaged to Fraulein de Ahna!' They married in autumn 1894.

The performances of *Guntram* went ahead, but the musicians were unhappy. It was described by the orchestra as 'this scourge of God', and the principal tenor demanded an increase in pension. Although it was only given one performance there were to be rich compensations for Strauss in the succession of superb orchestral tone-poems which he wrote after *Guntram* – *Till Eulenspiegel, Also sprach Zarathustra, Don Quixote* – and also in his family life when a son, Franz Alexander, was born in April 1897.

Offers from Berlin

By this time Strauss was increasingly sought after as a conductor and in 1898 received two offers of new posts – the chief conductorships of the Royal Court Opera in Berlin and the New York Philharmonic Orchestra. New York offered double the Berlin salary, but Berlin included generous holidays and pensions, and Strauss opted for the latter. Strauss never saw any virtue in starving in garrets, but although he was later charged with being obsessed with royalties, his interest in financial matters sprang from a genuine desire to see composing recognized as a profession. As he later remarked to his librettist Hugo von Hofmannsthal:

Strauss, his wife Pauline and their son Franz (above), in the villa at Garmisch. The villa, financed by royalties from the highly successful opera Salome, *was their home from 1908.*

ELEKTRA
VON
RICHARD STRAUSS
OP. 58.

Elektra, a one-act opera (original title page shown left), marked the beginning of Strauss's long collaboration with the Austrian poet and dramatist Hugo von Hofmannsthal, who wrote the librettos for this and many subsequent Strauss operas.

revelation in his next tone-poem, the *Symphonia Domestica* which was premièred during Strauss's first visit to the United States.

Prior to the performance he described it to the Press as 'a day in the life of my family, part lyrical, part humorous!' The humour within the music was more than matched by that directed at the piece from without. Furthermore, audiences confessed themselves embarrassed by Strauss's 'exploitation' of his private life.

The relationship between Richard and Pauline was a volatile one, with many a shouting match taking place before the public's bemused gaze. Most of the aggravation originated with Pauline, whose fiery temperament, lack of tact and, on occasion, down-right rudeness was in complete contrast to Richard's phlegmatic self-control. But the combination lasted. Once, after one of their notorious rows, Strauss remarked 'My wife's a bit rough sometimes, but that's what I need'.

'Salome' and 'Elektra'

Once settled in Berlin, Strauss's thoughts turned once again to opera. Strauss soon found an ideal subject: the legend of Salome provided a rich combination of the popular themes of sex, religion and oriental colour and had recently received a new and original interpretation in Oscar Wilde's play.

Salome was finished in 1904, but getting it staged proved almost as traumatic as *Guntram*. At the first rehearsal, all the singers handed back their parts and the leading lady almost backed out because of the 'indecent' eroticism of the Dance of the Seven Veils and the scene with Jokanaan's severed head. 'I won't do it — I'm a decent woman!' she protested. But despite these set-backs the opera went on and the first performance was a great success. Soon another 50 opera-houses were clamouring to perform it. There were problems with the censors in Vienna, and in New York, where there was such outrage at the first performance that the rest of the run had to be cancelled. But it made Strauss undeniably the most famous composer in Europe.

His next opera *Elektra*, was also fairly sensational, again dealing with a woman's obsession and revenge. For this work the librettist was the young playwright Hugo von Hofmannsthal. *Elektra* was only the beginning of a long and fruitful collaboration between playwright and composer.

Strauss's fame as the composer of *Salome* and *Elektra* was closely followed by his renown as a conductor, and, taking a year's leave of absence from the opera in Berlin in 1908, he travelled extensively, conducting in London, Vienna, St Petersburg and

Just prior to the summer of 1898, which he spent with his family at their former holiday home in Marquartstein (left), Strauss was offered the position of chief conductor to the Royal Court Opera in Berlin. Berlin (above) at that time was a wealthy cultural centre and in his memoirs Strauss recorded that 'on the whole my stay there was pure joy, and I found much appreciation and hospitality.'

One does not need to be a businessman to wish to derive decent remuneration after sitting up with a long opera score night after night for two or three years. Once the pleasure of creation has passed, then the annoyance of performances and those blessed criticisms begin, and only a good stipend can compensate one for that . . . I merely say out loud what other 'idealists' think to themselves.

His first composition in Berlin, the gigantic tone-poem *Ein Heldenleben* (A Hero's Life) met with a mixed reception. Being clearly autobiographical and including some substantial quotations from his own works, it earned for Strauss a reputation for arrogance and egocentricity, partly because a musical autobiography was considered 'tasteless'. But Strauss plunged even further into musical self-

Strauss's opera Salome was first performed in Dresden at the Court Theatre on 9 December 1905. The atmospheric set (right) designed for the première was by Emil Rieck, the Court Theatre's resident artist.

Paris as well as all over Germany. Also in 1908, the Strauss family settled into their newly-completed villa in Garmisch, which remained Richard's and Pauline's family home for the rest of their lives.

Successful as he already was, Strauss still had his greatest triumph in store. This was *Der Rosenkavalier*, Strauss's 'Mozart opera'. Like *Elektra*, it depended for its inspiration on Hofmannsthal's libretto, as Strauss acknowledged. The success of *Der Rosenkavalier* in Dresden was overwhelming. 50 performances were given within a year, with special trains ferrying eager audiences from Berlin. Other opera houses rushed to perform it as soon as Dresden's rights to the première had been fulfilled.

Strauss had now reached the peak of his career. Many fine stage works were to follow, but none that would compare with *Der Rosenkavalier's* enduring success. Indeed, his next collaboration with Hofmannsthal, *Ariadne auf Naxos*, met initially with failure. The ballet for Diaghilev and the Ballets Russes, *Josephslegende*, fared only a little better.

By this time Europe was on the verge of war, anti-German feeling was running high in England, and a few weeks after the assassination of Archduke Ferdinand at Sarajevo, Strauss was dismayed to learn that a large portion of his 30-years savings, deposited in London, had been confiscated. Strauss's attitude to world events was undeniably a selfish one. He viewed himself as an artist who should have the right to work undisturbed by political circumstances. His first reaction to the outbreak of war was of irritation at the financial inconvenience it caused him, followed by a genuine paternal concern for his son, Franz, whose delicate state of health eventually spared his being conscripted. His work, however, was interrupted as Hofmannsthal took up a diplomatic post and was frequently too busy to meet Strauss's needs with his customary speed.

With the end of the war, Strauss found himself at the crossroads in his life. He was aware that his music was fast becoming anachronistic – he had no real point of contact with the younger generation of composers, with Schoenberg, Stravinsky, Hindemith, or Bartók, for example. And in April 1918 Strauss's long association with the opera in Berlin came to an end, after a quarrel with the director. He was offered the post of Artistic Director at the Vienna Opera House. But when his appointment was announced, most of the opera-house's 800 staff demanded his withdrawal, claiming that his salary was excessive and that he would put on too many performances of his own operas. While the pro- and anti-Strauss factions in Vienna continued to bicker, Strauss

The costume of Princess Praline (right), designed for Strauss's ballet, Schlagobers (Whipped Cream), written as a tribute to Vienna.

The leading 'lights' of the Dresden Opera (below) which staged many of Strauss's premières. (Strauss is seated, centre; Hofmannsthal is standing at Strauss's right).

RZFELD ESDEN 1911
inspektor Hasait. Hofth. Maler Altenkirch Prof. Max Reinhardt Graf v. Seebach, Excellenz. Hugo v. Hofmannsthal. Prof. Roller. Dr. Richard Strauss. Prof. Fanto. General-Musikdirektor v. Schuch. Oberregisseur Toller.

himself remained in Garmisch, waiting for the fuss to die down. He eventually took up his appointment in Vienna on 1st December 1919.

At first everything went well, but soon relations in Vienna became strained. Not only was Strauss frequently absent, he was also in the habit of granting leave to singers to perform in his operas elsewhere – a practice which played havoc with the opera house's salary system. Strauss was unperturbed by such financial considerations, and retorted 'I am here to lose money'. The Press were also unhelpful, accusing him of turning the Opera into a Richard Strauss Theatre – although the number of performances of his own works was not, in fact, disproportionately high. By 1924, relations with the Vienna Opera had reached such a state that Strauss was forced to resign.

The rise of Nazism

Ever since World War 1, Strauss's output had been sparse. Now it dwindled almost to nothing, and the sudden death of Hofmannsthal in 1929 took away a close friend and a vital collaborator.

By 1931, Strauss had found another librettist in

Bildarchiv P.K.

Stefan Zweig (above) became Strauss's librettist from 1931, but their association was curtailed because Zweig was a Jew and Strauss, in his later years (right), was 'used' by the Nazis.

Bildarchiv Preussischer Kulturbesitz

Österreichische Nationalbibliothek

Princess Pralinée

Stefan Zweig and the two started work on an adaptation of Ben Jonson's *The silent woman*. But Zweig was a Jew, and Hitler's rise to power in Germany had begun. Many artists chose to leave Germany; Strauss stayed partly because he felt politics had nothing to do with him and partly, perhaps, because he wanted to protect his own Jewish daughter-in-law Alice. Whatever the truth, he has been heavily criticised for his tacit acceptance of the Nazi regime and his music is still banned in Israel. Perhaps his worst 'crime' was to conduct *Parsifal* at Bayreuth on the 50th anniversary of Wagner's death – after Toscanini pulled out. Naturally, the Nazis made the most of Strauss's apparent endorsement of their regime and in 1933, Goebbels appointed him president of the new State Music Bureau.

At this time, Strauss was still working with Zweig, ignoring the political situation. Soon theatres were forbidden to produce works by Jews and when the news of his collaboration with a Jew got out, there was, ironically, a public scandal. Strauss was forced to write to the authorities begging to be allowed to continue his devotion to German culture without resorting to politics. In 1935, he received a state questionnaire which requested the names of two witnesses to his professional ability. He wrote 'Mozart and Richard Wagner'. He was asked to resign from the State Music Bureau – a strange irony, since he had never asked to join in the first place.

As Europe plunged into war once more, Strauss continued to compose and right in the middle of the worst conflict, in 1942, created his most successful work for 30 years, the opera *Capriccio*. There followed a stream of quiet introspective music that did much to restore his fading reputation. But his health was fading too now, and on 8 September 1949, he died, commenting, 'Dying is just as I composed it in *Tod und Verklärung*.'

Tone poems

In his tone poems – the most celebrated of all his orchestral works – Strauss uses the orchestra to masterly effect, creating for the listener a series of vivid musical pictures.

From the mighty apocalyptic sunrise that opens *Also sprach Zarathustra* to the jaunty merriment of Till's street ditty in *Till Eulenspiegel,* Richard Strauss's music in these, his most famous orchestral works, is remarkably real – so real that every sound, every passage seems to conjure up a very clear picture. The effect is that the orchestra builds up a series of images to tell a story in music. They are musical poems or, as Strauss described them, *Tondichtung,* sound or 'tone' poems.

The idea of approaching symphonic music in such a realistic way was not new. Indeed, it had been developing among the more progressive composers throughout the Romantic era. In the search for a more expressive way of writing music to replace the abandoned classical forms, composers such as Liszt and Wagner advocated a dramatic treatment of music – music was to be just a vehicle for the expression of ideas and emotions. Franz Liszt in particular had developed the 'symphonic poem',

Till Eulenspiegel is the central character of Strauss's tone poem of the same name. A legendary lovable rogue, he is characterized by the witty and jovial image of the carousing violinist (left).

The music echoes 'Till's' passage through all his adventures. At one point Till, who can change his appearance at will, appears as a gallant young man exchanging pleasantries with any pretty girl who crosses his path (right).

a symphony which was held together not by the rigid classical four movement form but by an extra-musical and, commonly, literary idea. In a way, it paralleled the growing interest in 'programme music' initiated by Berlioz's *Symphonie Fantastique,* music which followed a specific programme to recreate a story, an image, or an idea in purely musical terms.

Strauss's tone poems are really the natural and inevitable combination of these two strands in progressive Romantic music. Progressive composers rejected the idea of 'absolute' music and the classical belief that form alone is enough. They believed the music must carry ideas.

Strauss himself made a brilliant reputation throughout Europe in the 1890s as the leader of the 'moderns' with his sensational, dramatic tone poems. The 1890s were without question the era of the tone poem, and Strauss's immensely varied works were incomparably the most significant contribution to the genre.

'Till Eulenspiegels lustige Streiche'

Strauss's title means 'Till Eulenspiegel's Merry Pranks'. Till Eulenspiegel was a popular figure of medieval German folklore, a practical joker who played

tricks on everyone from the king down to the humblest peasant. Strauss had encountered this character in Kistler's opera about him and in a recent new edition of the tale. This historical Till Eulenspiegel was the son of a peasant who died of the Black Death in 1350, but it was his legendary caricature rather than the reality that inspired Strauss to write his own opera on Till. Strauss eventually gave up the idea of an opera, but by the time he did he had already completed, on 6 May 1895, a purely instrumental treatment of the subject. We have to disagree with the comment written by Strauss's wife Pauline in the margin of one of the sketches for Till – 'horrid composing', she wrote. 'Observation by my lady wife' wrote Strauss alongside it. But whatever his wife thought, the public loved it and the audience for the première in Cologne on 5 November 1895 gave *Till Eulenspiegel* a rousing reception. Although the critics were divided Till soon made his way round other cities, and the press were forced to concede his lovable qualities in the face of enthusiastic public support.

Programme notes

When Strauss was asked to provide a programme analysis for its première he declined, but later on gave some indication of the meaning of the various episodes. The gentle opening on the violins is of course 'Once upon a time there was a lovable rogue . . .' with a delightful solo horn theme, the rogue immediately puts his head round the door, checks the coast is clear and announces himself again with more confidence:

Example 1

This rapidly builds up to a climax and, after a loud sustained chord on horns and strings, Till's lively second theme emerges on the clarinet, meaning *Das war ein arger Kobold* ('He was a wicked rascal').

These two themes are developed in a section marked 'up to new tricks'. The writing here is kaleidoscopic and Strauss seems to revel in his prodigious skill at creating spectacular effects with his very large orchestra.

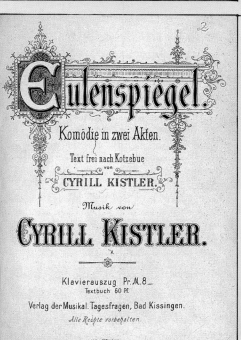

Strauss was inspired to write Till Eulenspiegel's Merry Pranks *after he attended a performance of Cyrill Kistler's opera,* Eulenspiegel, *the title page of which is shown above.*

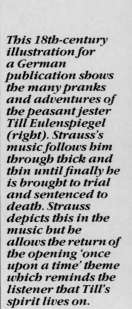

This 18th-century illustration for a German publication shows the many pranks and adventures of the peasant jester Till Eulenspiegel (right). Strauss's music follows him through thick and thin until finally he is brought to trial and sentenced to death. Strauss depicts this in the music but he allows the return of the opening 'once upon a time' theme which reminds the listener that Till's spirit lives on.

Jean-Coup Charmet

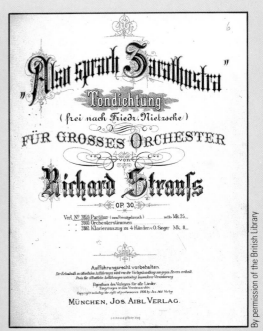

The first true episode is launched with a sudden discord and a cymbal crash. 'Hop! On horseback straight through the market-women' gallops Till, creating orchestral havoc as he goes. Presumably he is unhorsed since he makes his escape with descending strides on the trombones which say 'He runs away in seven-league boots'. The quiet, diffident flecks of woodwind tone that follow give us (and Till) a moment's respite and represent Till 'hidden in a mousehole'.

Undaunted, Till soon emerges for another adventure, and a new tune on the violas, steady of gait and ingratiating of manner, shows Till 'disguised as a parson, oozing unction and morality'. Alas, the disguise is less than perfect for the sudden emergence of Till's second tune on clarinet indicates 'the rogue peeping out of his big toe', and only five bars later the muted horns, muted trumpets and five solo violins quietly intimate that Till is engaged in a dangerous practice – 'seized with a sudden horror of his end because of his mockery of religion' Till desists.

A long, rapid downward scale on the solo violin sweeps Till into his next adventure, with 'Till as gallant, exchanging courtesies with pretty girls'. Till soon warms to his task of seduction until he is tactfully rejected, but 'however delicate, a rejection is still a rejection' and Till's wrath breaks out as his themes stride around the orchestra and four horns furiously 'vow to take revenge on all mankind'.

Till's next adventure is with the Philistines, whose motif is given to four bassoons and bass clarinet and has an appropriate sobriety. 'After he has imposed a few atrocious themes on them, he abandons them, baffled, to their fate' and in a savage crescendo Till reveals himself (second theme) and 'grimaces from a distance'. This bitter mockery dissolves into 'Till's street ditty', a jaunty carefree tune which fades away as Till swiftly moves off the scene.

A strange, ghostly interlude follows as Strauss allows us to get our breath back before the next adventure. There are in fact no more programmatic incidents in the music from now until the end. There is instead an extended recapitulation of the earlier music. Its increasingly tumultuous character implies that Till is becoming ever more reckless and at the climax of this passage the theme of Till's mockery of religion is blasted out. The riot is dramatically cut off and Till is brought to trial as long, slow, loud trombone chords (the judges) alternate with Till's cheeky clarinet theme. Even this, it seems, is just another adventure to Till, but it is his last –

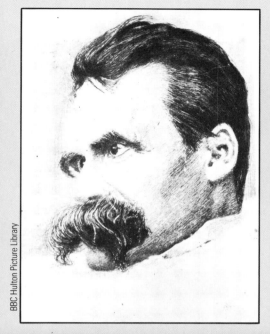

with a forceful wide descending interval, the brass announce the verdict, hanging. (*Der Tod!* – 'Death' Strauss marked the two notes of this phrase.) 'Up the ladder! There he swings, the air is squeezed out of him, a final jerk. Till's mortal part is gone.' This gruesome scene is vividly depicted by Strauss, but he is too good a storyteller to leave us with moistened eyes. In an epilogue the 'once upon a time' theme returns, as if to remind us that it was only a story. With a final flourish, Till leaves the stage and slams the door behind him.

Also sprach Zarathustra op. 30

Also sprach Zarathustra was inspired by Nietzsche's notorious book of the same name. In this Nietzsche uses the 7th century BC Persian mystic, Zoroaster, (or Zarathustra) as a vehicle for his own views. Zarathustra the prophet lives alone in the mountains, but descends among men from time to time to give them the benefit of his wisdom. His principal target is the naive

belief in a comforting religion which blesses the meek, and his principal doctrine is that of the *Übermensch* or Superman. Zarathustra gives his views on many issues and each chapter ends with the words *Also sprach Zarathustra* (Thus spoke Zarathustra). These ideas were regarded by artists of the time as an exciting, liberating influence, and Strauss was no exception. But he did not subscribe to all Nietzsche's philosophy. Instead, he took the principal themes of *Zarathustra* as a starting point for his tone-poem, selecting some of Nietzsche's chapter headings to head the eight sections of his score.

The first performances were a success with audiences but not with critics. They dismissed it as 'this feeble work' or 'a huge success — as a joke'. Strauss had to explain that this was not to be regarded as 'philosophy set to music' and pointed to his subtitle 'Symphonic poem, *freely* after Friedrich Nietzsche'.

Also sprach Zarathustra (title page above left) was written immediately after Till Eulenspiegel. It was inspired by the German philosopher Nietzsche's notorious book of the same name. Nietzsche (above) was a self-styled 'anti-Christ' and many citizens of imperial Germany found his philosophies unacceptable. Although Strauss did not subscribe fully to Nietzsche's views he took the main ideas of the book as the starting point for his tone poem.

In the section 'Of Great Longing' Strauss expresses man's eternal struggle to free himself from superstition which inevitably brings him into conflict with the elemental and overwhelming power of nature (left).

The hallowed and unemotional atmosphere of the classical School of Athens (right) seems to sum up Strauss's attempt to express in music the aridity of pure academic learning.

In Don Juan, *Strauss brilliantly captured the emotions of the legendary woman-hunter (far right).*

Programme notes

The opening of *Also sprach Zarathustra* is one of the most imposing beginnings in the whole of music – yet it is made from the simplest of musical materials. It depicts Zarathustra's address to the rising sun.

With an organ holding the note C, four trumpets announce the dawn of a new spirit with the most fundamental notes in Western music (a leap to the octave via the dominant):

Example 2

This is repeated twice, each time followed by dramatic full orchestra chords and thundering timpani strokes building to a mighty climax. The organ is left holding the climactic chord after the orchestra has stopped, and the section headed *Of the Backworldsmen* about primitive religious faith begins groping at first, then developing to the 'credo' theme on the horn, and richly scored climax on strings. The following section, *Of the great Longing* shows man struggling to free himself from superstition and fighting against nature (Ex. 2 on English horn). Zarathustra stirs himself as a scale on the harp sweeps us into *Joys and Passions* where the music quickens and the surging main theme suggests the restlessness of man's emotional life. At the climax, a new theme, the theme of disgust, is hurled into the texture by the protesting trombones. *The Song of the Grave* that follows uses the same material, but in a veiled and shadowy texture that implies that the passions are only man's way of turning his thoughts from his inevitable fate. But this exhausted, sinking sensation is pierced by Ex. 2 on the trumpet at the peak of this episode.

Next comes the dry, academic fugue *Of Learning,* only to be brushed aside as once more the music soars up into a dance of rushing high strings and upper woodwinds. But the escape is foiled, and the fugue breaks out again in *The Convalescent* with Zarathustra's sickness and near madness, giving way to a new insight into his mission.

'Up, abysmal thought, from the depths! I am thy cock, thy dawn . . .' Zarathustra stirs himself once more, and Strauss takes us right up into the highest reaches of the orchestra with trilling flights from flutes and piccolos and a cock crow from the trumpet. This frenzied, light-headed music leads us at last to the Superman and his 'Tanz-lied' or Dance-song – the most statement of Ex. 2 sweeps us up to the climax of the dance, when the waltz tune is heard at breathtaking speed and the first stroke of the Midnight Bell rings out. This is the climax leading to *'The Night Wanderer's Song'*, and as each successive stroke of the bell gets softer, Zarathustra warns his disciples of life's complexity.

The music winds down into an exquisite epilogue, as Man finds peace at last. But it is not an untroubled peace, and a restless swinging between high and low chords of the last pages suggest that the searching must continue.

Don Juan op. 20

For a 24 year old composer, *Don Juan* is a work of the most audacious mastery. It was a brilliant success at its first performance in Weimar in 1889, and established Strauss as the most important composer in Germany.

Strauss chose a verse play by Nikolaus Lenau as the basis of his work about the legendary woman-hunter; his pursuit of pleasure and his ultimate disillusion and willing embracing of death.

Programme notes

The tone-poem begins with an upward rush on the strings as Don Juan leaps into action with one of the most difficult of virtuoso openings in the orchestral repertoire. The trumpet rides above the tumult with the Don's main theme and he arrives at his first brief flirtation as soon as the music becomes tranquil,. But clearly this tiny capricious flute phrase is not a serious claim on our hero, who is soon genuinely smitten and drawn by the solo violin into an extended love scene.

The passion now spent, the cellos stir Juan back into action. A new conquest is not far away though, and this time the Don is quite besotted by one of the longest and loveliest of all solos for the oboe.

controversial moment in a controversial work, for the dance is none other than a Viennese waltz! Even today critics find this hard to accept, but it is entirely in keeping with the ironic, mocking tone common to the work of both Nietzsche and Strauss.

Example 3

The music becomes ever more intoxicating and merges into a development section which has no Nietzschean heading in the score but reviews all the previous motifs in a bewildering series of keys and thematic combinations. At last a tremendous

Raphael 'School of Athens'. Vatican, Rome/The Bridgeman Art Library

Molly Benatar 'Heart Throb'. Fine Art Photographic Library

Understanding music: heroes in music

A large part of the programme music of the last 200 years is devoted to the musical portrayal of famous characters, or heroes. Just why certain characters became such attractive subjects for composers is not hard to appreciate. History, legend and literature are full of popular heroes and these characters provide ideal ready-made themes for the composer to interpret in music.

The great romantic heroes of literature, particularly, caught the imagination of the Romantic composers and it was they who took the hero theme to the peak of expressiveness. The notion of an unfettered spirit, striving against the strictures of a conventional society, or one lacking understanding, fitted perfectly their desire to use music as a vehicle for expressing intense, and often highly personal, emotion and feelings. Some heroes, especially the ill-fated or tragic, crop up time and time again in the music of the Romantic composers and in the literary works of Lord Byron, Scott, Goethe, Schiller and Shakespeare they found a rich source of material.

The idea of taking a hero as a theme, however, had begun long before the Romantics. Telemann, for instance, the prolific Baroque composer, wrote a programme overture called *Don Quixote* which, like Richard Strauss's tone poem of the same name, shows the comic adventures of the old knight and his comrade, and is one of the earliest examples of a hero in music.

Shakespeare's works provided many 'heroes' which Romantic composers, particularly, drew on. Strauss, too, found a hero in Macbeth *(below) for his tone poem of 1888.*

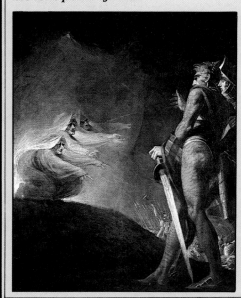

Later, Schumann wrote the overture *Manfred* for a production of Byron's verse drama *Manfred*. In this work Schumann portrays a typical romantic, Byronic hero – a sensitive, sensual intellectual, exiled by destiny or a reactionary society, to brood on the vagaries of fate in solitary splendour. Such a theme allowed Schumann to pour out his musical character portrait in an emotive, highly descriptive way.

Manfred also inspried a lengthy symphony, full of invention and orchestral colour, from Tchaikovsky. The doom-laden Manfred appealed to the Russian composer who used fatalism as a theme a number of times.

Shakespearean heroes dominated a whole section of the Romantics' orchestral repertoire. *Hamlet,* as seen by the Romantics, was in many ways a similar character to Manfred, and it is not surprising to find Tchaikovsky using the Prince of Denmark as the hero of another orchestral work. Tchaikovsky's *Romeo and Juliet Fantasy Overture* is also one of the most famous musical interpretations of the Shakespearean tragedy of youthful star-crossed love.

Berlioz, yet another composer who looked toward the Romantic hero, also created a musical work on the Romeo and Juliet theme – a vast symphony with soloists and chorus. He was similarly entranced by the tragic *King Lear* for which he wrote an overture. Schumann wrote his overture, *Julius Caesar* in 1851, and even Dvořák was drawn to a tragic representation of the passions of *Othello,* although the title was subsequently changed. Nearer to our own time, Elgar has brilliantly represented the anti-hero, Sir John Falstaff.

Even amidst these dominant Shakespearean characters, the romantic love of, and sympathy with, any man outside society is evident. So it was to Byron that Berlioz looked when he portrayed *Harold in Italy*. This is a symphony based upon the Italian incidents in Byron's autobiographical *Childe Harold's Pilgrimmage.*

The great and gloomy romantic heroes inspired the Nationalists too, though the historical and native folk-heroes of their homelands provided extra material. Janacek's *Taras Bulba,* Wagner's *Siegfried,* Gliere's gigantic *Ilya Mourometz* symphony, and a series of tone poems by Sibelius, Dvořák and Smetana added to the legacy of the hero in music.

What we are left with in all these works is not only a musical portrait gallery of heroes, but also revealing pictures of the composers themselves.

This section has a most beautiful coda for muted strings and low flutes, music of emotional contentment. Then the strings rush up once more to a high trill and we see Don Juan in all his splendour, announced by a horn theme which once heard, is never forgotten:

Example 4

A playful episode for wind and trumpet with a tingling glockenspiel part leads Don Juan into the carnival, his heroic theme

Fresh from his last conquest Don Juan moves on to the next diversion – a carnival (above) where in the midst of gaiety he falls into despair.

(Ex. 4) riding high in the trumpet above the swirling strings. But the Don falls into despair. As a joke before embarking on his final adventure he invites the statue of a nobleman he has killed to supper, but his 'guest' turns from stone into a man of flesh and blood – the nobleman's son, bent on a duel to the death. The music becomes ever more frenzied, until Don Juan emerges as clearly superior. But with victory in his grasp, the libertine's fatal sense of satiety and disillusionment overcomes him. He drops his guard and lets his adversary run him through, and a stab of dissonance from the trumpet fixes the precise moment. Immediately, Juan's life shivers away in string tremolandi, and two plucked string chords close the work with the bitter emptiness of Don Juan's final moments.

FURTHER LISTENING

Eine Alpensinfonie, op. 64

By the outbreak of World War I it was generally thought that Strauss had abandoned his orchestral writing in favour of opera. But in 1915 Strauss produced this 'symphonic' work, which he saw as a simple and direct tone picture of the joys of mountain scenery. A single hearing of the work is sufficient to show the enormous amount of craft and sophistication and the brilliant orchestration of what is more a series of pictures than a symphony itself. What the listener is left with is a dramatic and convincing portrayal of nature which is as attractive to the ear as any of Strauss's more profound works.

Tod und Verklärung, op. 24

This work is one of Strauss's earliest orchestral masterpieces, redolent with *fin de siècle* atmosphere. Here, for the first time, he was not just illustrating a chosen text, but attempting to depict musically the longing for death and oblivion of a man who is content to let go of life and, in reflection, recalls past events by way of resignation. The atmosphere is superbly created by Strauss, whose imagination was obviously fired by his subject matter.

Vier letzte Lieder, op. posth.

At the close of his life, when all his operas lay behind him, Strauss felt capable only of songs. For this we may count ourselves lucky, for these are four of the most beautiful and moving orchestral lieder ever written. Each piece has a wonderful poignancy, with the simple, heartfelt resignation to mortality and destiny underlined by translucent orchestral colours and soaring vocal lines.

IN THE BACKGROUND

'Der Führer'

From the economic, social and political chaos of post-World War I Germany rose a man with a single-minded vision of a 'New Order' – Adolf Hitler.

The burning of the German Parliament (The Reichstag) was a significant step towards Hitler's consolidation of power. The Brown Book of the Hitler Terror, published at the time of the Reichstag Fire Trial by opponents of Hitler's National Socialists, owed much of its impact to the photomontages of John Heartfield. One such illustration (left) showed Hermann Goering as a blood-spattered butcher, standing in front of the burning Reichstag with an axe. The implication is plain: the Nazis began the fire themselves, to give them an excuse to shed Communist blood. Today, it is widely believed that Joseph Goebbels, the Nazi propaganda minister, devised the plan. The perpetrators gained access to the Reichstag through a tunnel leading from Hermann Goering's official residence.

A campaign poster of the 1932 elections (right) claimed that von Hindenburg, incumbent president and hero of the Great War, was the only lifeline to a Germany being pulled under by Communists, Nazis and other factions. But in 1932 Hindenburg was already 85, and out of control of such factions. Although he won the election, it was only one year before he was pressurized into offering the post of Chancellor to Hitler.

On the night of 27 February 1933, Adolf Hitler was at dinner with his Minister of Public Enlightenment and Propaganda, Joseph Goebbels. He had been Chancellor for just four weeks. Suddenly, the meal was interrupted by a frantic telephone call: the Reichstag – the German Parliament – was on fire! At first Goebbels refused to believe the message, but eventually he and his guest drove to the scene.

Rumours of arson were rife among prominent Nazis. The fire, they said, was a final attempt by Communists to strike a crippling blow at democracy and to seize power in the ensuing atmosphere of panic. An eye-witness recalled Hitler's reaction:

On a balcony stood Hitler, surrounded by a band of his faithful followers. Hitler was leaning over the stone parapet, gazing at the red ocean of fire. Then he swung towards us. I saw that his face had turned quite scarlet, both with excitement and with the heat . . . Suddenly he started screaming at the top of his voice, 'Now we'll show them. Anyone who stands in our way will be shot, mown down. The German people have been soft too long. All Communist MPs must be hanged this very night. All friends of the Communists must be locked up!'

Later, a British journalist overheard the Chancellor privately expressing doubts as to the causes of the fire. But Hitler was aware of the propaganda value that blaming the Communists would have. Communism was a serious rival to his own political viewpoint – the politics of Nazism – and if any mud might stick, it was worth flinging – particularly as general elections were less than a week away.

In the official Prussian State Government announcement the following day the blame was laid squarely at the feet of the Communists – the 'most monstrous act of terrorism so far carried out by Communism in Germany'. What followed was a Nazi rampage of terror against Communists and Communist sympathisers that ultimately consolidated Hitler's personal power and set Germany on the road to war.

Trial and verdict

The police eventually charged a Dutch worker called Marinus van der Lubbe with causing the fire. He confessed to arson but always maintained that the fire was a personal protest against Hitler, involving no one but himself. However, this was unacceptable to the Nazis, who wished to stage a show trial with Communism in the dock. So three Communists, including the prominent Bulgarian exile Georgi Dimitrov, were also alongside van der Lubbe, as fellow conspirators. Van der Lubbe was condemned and beheaded, but insufficient evidence against the others resulted in their acquittal.

Dimitrov actually succeeded in using the trial to launch a Communist counter-attack, arguing that the Nazis and not the Communists had started the fire. This view gained international credence thanks to a campaign by supporters of the defendants and anti-Fascists, both inside and outside Germany. One of the campaign's publications, appearing in various

languages, was *The Brown Book of the Hitler Terror.* A powerful feature of this book was the anti-Nazi artwork by John Heartfield. Heartfield – a German who had adopted an English name – was famous for developing *Photomontage,* pasting photographs together to create a visual message. Heartfield's pictures remain as some of the most powerful images charting the rise of Hitler.

But the Nazis had not invited the world's press to their show trial to witness acquittals, let alone Communist propaganda from the dock. However, the fire and the trial, fanned by Nazi rhetoric, did create enough hysteria to convince the German population

The dangerous invective of **Mein Kampf,** *right, which Hitler wrote in prison at Landsberg, might have passed unnoticed. But Hitler, when he received a public platform, had all the charisma of an evangelical preacher and his book took on the status of a Nazi Bible.*

Hitler was entertaining gullible Germans to 'bread and circuses', as the cartoon (centre) from a satirical magazine of the time implies. Crowd reactions to his rhetoric were indistinguishable from crowd reactions to a circus entertainer.

An important factor in explaining Hitler's rise is Germany's economic state in the 1920s-30s. Inflation had reached nightmare levels. Workers were paid by the day in millions of marks (far right, top) and ran from factory to shop to spend them before the next wave of inflation rendered their baseless currency worthless.

The contemporary pictures of Otto Dix provide a glimpse of pre-Nazi Berlin where decadence and permissiveness ran riot in a broken, degenerate society (far right, bottom). To rural and provincial Germany, Berlin displayed the worst symptoms of Germany in decay. And Hitler's promise to destroy it and restore national pride seemed an attractive proposition to many Germans.

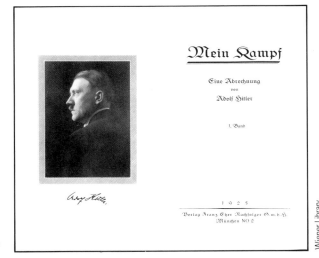

that Communism posed a threat and that Hitler's right wing Nationalism could lead them confidently forward to a better future. Consequently, the Nazis won the general election on 5 March, but by a margin too small to satisfy Hitler. He proposed an Enabling Act giving him powers to draft a bill and make it law within 24 hours – without having to fight opposition in the Reichstag. To encourage his opponents (and any dissenters within his own party) to vote for the Act, Nazi storm-troopers saturated the Reichstag building. Outside, Nazi supporters chanted, 'We want the bill – or fire and murder!'

The bill was passed. In effect, the parliamentary democracy which Germany had enjoyed since the end of World War I had been replaced by an extreme right-wing one-party dictatorship. Soon all parties except the Nazis were banned, and free elections ceased – Fascism reigned supreme. When President Hindenburg died the following year, Hitler did not appoint a successor. Instead, he made himself the head of the German state, with the new title of Führer (Leader).

With hindsight it is perhaps too easy to condemn Germany's acceptance of this situation, knowing, as we do, the eventual outcome in the horrors of World War II. But a brief glimpse back to pre-Nazi Germany shows all too many reasons for the meteoric rise in popularity of Hitler and his brand of National Socialism.

The beer-hall putsch

Only ten years before the Reichstag fire Hitler had been serving a humiliating jail sentence in the fortress at Landsberg, Bavaria. This was the result of trying to gain power by force, a tactic Hitler claimed to have learned from his Communist rivals:

The Marxists taught – if you will not be my brother, I will bash your skull in. Our motto shall be – if you will not be a true German, I will bash your skull in. For we are convinced that we cannot succeed without a struggle. We have to fight with ideas, but if necessary, with our fists.

At first, conflict was limited to pitched street battles between Communists and Socialists. But in 1923, inspired by the Fascist Benito Mussolini's seizure of power in Italy the previous year, Hitler attempted a military *putsch* (coup).

The plan was to seize the State Government of Bavaria, before making an advance on Berlin. The rising began with a Nazi attack on a Munich beer hall

BBC Hulton Picture Library

Library of Congress/MacClancy Collection

Before Hitler could gain complete political control he had to destroy support for his Communist rivals. Here, his 'Brownshirts' parade in the streets with banners proclaiming, 'Death to Marxism'. Rosa Luxemburg (above) – a leading Communist – was beaten to death along with fellow Communist Karl Leibknecht, and their bodies dumped in a canal shortly after the suppression of a Communist uprising in Berlin.

Hitler's second target after Communism was the Jew. But he went beyond heaping the blame for Germany's economic plight on Jewish shoulders in rousing the basest, most barbaric instincts of his followers: the lust to humiliate and brutalize a defenceless section of society which, out of ignorance and jealousy, was widely mistrusted. In the streets of Vienna in 1938 the Hitler Youth 'supervise' the scrubbing of a street by its Jewish inhabitants (top right).

Hitler chose to lump together Judaism and Communism as common enemies of Germany, as witnessed by this huge racist poster depicting 'The Wandering Jew' (bottom right). 'Wandering' implied that the Jewish heart, fixed on its spiritual homeland, could never be loyal to Germany. There could be no such thing as a German Jew.

in which prominent Bavarian politicians were holding a meeting. Hitler's National Socialist troops, carrying guns, flooded the beer hall. Waving a revolver, Hitler pushed his way through the crowd. He jumped on a table and fired two shots into the ceiling, demanding quiet. He then announced the removal of the Bavarian and national governments, and proclaimed himself in charge as a provisional replacement. He then proposed a march on Berlin.

The next day, Hitler led a march through Munich, accompanied by General Ludendorff, a hero of the Great War. Ludendorff had espoused a religious revival of Germanic paganism, which involved the worship of Wotan, and rabid anti-Semitism. Such beliefs fitted admirably with Hitler's vision, of course, and this old Imperial general was to be Chief of Staff in Hitler's new Germany.

The dream ended when the Bavarian police opened fire on the marchers. Many were killed, but Hitler was saved when his bodyguard threw himself on his master, his body receiving 11 bullets. Hitler, suffering only a dislocated shoulder, was arrested along with Ludendorff.

At his trial, Hitler was unrepentant. He predicted a time when his Nazis and those who had fired on them in Munich would be united, and he confidently appealed to a higher court of justice:

You may pronounce us guilty a thousand times over, but the goddess of the eternal court of history will smile and tear to tatters . . . the sentence of this court. For she acquits me.

The famous war hero Ludendorff was acquitted, but Hitler was sentenced to five years in prison, the minimum sentence for treason. He only served nine months, in rather comfortable surroundings, and used the opportunity to write *Mein Kampf* (My Struggle). This was a catalogue of invective against weak government and Jews rather than a sound

political philosophy, but it was later to become the Nazi Bible.

The legal road to power
The failure of armed insurrection prompted Hitler to consider the ballot-box, instead of force, as an alternative route to power. In a letter from prison he reluctantly admitted, 'We shall have to hold our noses and enter the Reichstag'.

But the Nazis did not bother to conceal their cynical attitude to democracy. The party newspaper *Der Angriff* (Attack), edited by Joseph Goebbels, a prominent member of the party, openly explained:

We enter Parliament in order to supply ourselves in the arsenal of democracy with its own weapons . . . If democracy is so stupid as to give us free meal tickets and salaries for the purpose, that is its affair . . . We come as enemies.

But legal electioneering was only part of the Nazis' way of overcoming opposition – street thuggery and terror was the other way. The English writer Christopher Isherwood was in Berlin in the early thirties, and chillingly described the ways in which the *Sturmabteilung* (the SA – the brownshirted members of the Nazi party) terrorized the population:

Almost every evening, the SA men come into the cafe. Sometimes they are only collecting money; everybody is compelled to give something. Sometimes they have come to make an 'arrest'. One evening, a Jewish writer who was present ran into the telephone box to ring up the police. The Nazis dragged him out, and he was taken away. Nobody moved a finger. You could have heard a pin drop till they were gone.

A favourable tide
The Nazi readiness to use the jackboot, though, does not wholly explain the swing in the electoral

his friend Christopher Isherwood. But they repulsed Adolf Hitler, and in his eyes Berlin displayed the degeneracy which he saw as symptomatic of a sick Germany. He called Berlin 'that sinful Babel'.

In this libertarian atmosphere, the arts flourished. Indeed, many of the surviving impressions of life in the 'Roaring Twenties' come from drawings and paintings of Berlin life by satirical artists like Otto Dix and George Grosz. The Nazis opposed such trends. Innovations were condemned as 'culturally Bolshevist', 'Jewish' or 'degenerate'.

Once in power, Nazi policy towards painters and painting was typical of their overall attitude to the arts. Unacceptable artists, personnel and paintings were purged from art academies and museums. At least 16,000 examples of 'degenerate art' were confiscated from Germany's major collections. Many were burnt at the headquarters of the Berlin fire brigade in 1939.

Out of 1,400 artists condemned, 112 were singled

fortunes of the party. In the mid-1920s, the National Socialist German Workers' Party was of minor importance in the Reichstag, gaining only 12 out of 490 seats in the 1928 election. Yet by 1932 the Nazis had 230 seats, the largest single-party in parliament. This popularity was reaffirmed in 1933, after the Reichstag fire. Such a dramatic triumph, reached largely by constitutional means, can be attributed to genuine, widespread and seething public discontent with the existing state of affairs within Germany.

After World War 1 Germany had been 'punished' for starting it. The victors had demanded crippling reparation payments and snatched up whatever borderlands they could. The economy was broken by the cost of war, and the Weimar Republic was a signal failure. Germans felt humiliated, robbed, unloved and isolated.

A New Order

Many Germans were attracted to Nazi promises of a 'New Order'. At the centre of this mystical vision was a determination to restore national pride and to punish those held responsible for German humiliation. This involved a ferocious assault on the peace settlement after the Great War, and another on the 'degenerate' culture that had since flourished in the desperate times which followed.

Berlin, particularly, had gained a legendary reputation as a city of sexual permissiveness and gay nightlife, vividly recalled by the Austrian writer Stefan Zweig:

Made-up boys with artificial waistlines promenaded along the Kurfurstendamm . . . and in the darkened bars one could see high public officials and high financiers courting drunken sailors without shame. Even the Rome of Suetonius had not known orgies like the Berlin transvestite balls . . . Young ladies proudly boasted that they were perverted; to be suspected of virginity at sixteen would have been considered a disgrace in every school in Berlin.

These phenomena held a grim fascination for foreign observers like the English writers W. H. Auden and

GROSSE POLITISCHE SCHAU IM BIBLIOTHEKSBAU DES DEUTSCHEN MUSEUMS ZU MÜNCHEN · AB 8. NOVEMBER 1937 · TÄGLICH GEÖFFNET VON 10-21 UHR

out for humiliation. The infamous 'Degenerate Art' Exhibition opened in Munich in 1937. The works were deliberately presented in a chaotic way, with insulting captions. An accompanying catalogue hurled abuse at the exhibits, supported by the Fuhrer's invective on the subject of modern artists. He proposed one of two institutions for these painters – the hospital or the criminal court.

At the same time, in Munich, the Nazis presented their alternative to modern art in a specially constructed House of German Art. The exhibits were overwhelmingly figurative and elevating, seeking to promote a positive image of the German nation. There was a particular emphasis on healthy rural life, intended to contrast with Berlin.

Communist scapegoats and Jewish whipping-boys

Because of the economic collapse and mass unemployment caused by war reparations and the worldwide Depression of 1929 to 1931, there was an eager readiness to listen to Nazi rhetoric about creating a 'Thousand Year Reich' and regenerating Germany. In 1922 the mark was relatively worthless on the world money-markets: 162 to the dollar. By 1923, due to the appalling policy of printing bank notes to conceal national bankruptcy, the exchange rate was 4,200,000,000,000 marks to the dollar! Nazis presented themselves as saviours to big and small businesses facing bankruptcy and to blue- and white-collar workers facing unemployment. There is an important correlation between increasing unemployment and votes for the Nazis. And Hitler, when he came to power, *did* reconstruct the economy, restoring the mark to international credibility. He also instigated massive job-creation schemes – building autobahns, for example.

Above all, the Nazis were able to convince many that they had identified the cause of post-War economic calamities – the Communist and the Jew.

Well-off Germans had been terrified of Communism ever since Lenin and the Bolsheviks seized power in Russia in 1917. Communist parties had been formed throughout the world. The German Communist Party was formed in 1919, and almost immediately a Communist uprising was staged in Berlin, but it was bloodily suppressed by the government. One of the leaders, Rosa Luxemburg, regarded this defeat as a temporary setback:

Order reigns in Berlin! You stupid lackeys! Your 'order' is built on sand. Tomorrow the revolution will rear its head once again!

Shortly after writing this, Luxemburg and another Communist leader were beaten to death and dumped in a Berlin canal by a group of ex-soldiers working for the government.

Nevertheless, the Communists were an important force in German politics throughout the 1920s and 1930s. Indeed, they became the most popular party in Berlin, giving it the nickname 'Red City'. But Berlin was not Germany, and many Germans sympathized with Nazi opposition to the 'Red Menace'.

Anti-Semitism

The Jew was the second scapegoat to be singled out by the Nazis. Indeed, 'Jew', 'Communist' and 'Marxist' were often used as interchangeable insults by Hitler:

If with the help of his Marxist creed, the Jew is victorious over the other peoples of the world, his

crown will be the funeral wreath of humanity ... by defending myself against the Jew, I am fighting for the work of the Lord.*

In reality, Hitler abhorred the 'pity-ethic' of Christianity and sought to oust it with a revival of pagan rites and festivals. The blonde-haired goddesses and war-hungry warrior-gods of the old Teutonic religion would be much more amenable to his predatory foreign policies and his plans for building an Aryan Master-Race. Still, the Catholic Church was too influential to antagonize. So Hitler assured it that it was in no way under threat – then proceeded to rob it of much of its income and power.

Anti-Semitism was confined neither to the Nazis nor to Germany. Just before World War I, for example, Jews were persecuted in a number of countries, especially Russia, where Christian terrorists murdered up to 50,000 between 1905 and 1909.

Chaste and wholesome, the girl in the poster (above) embodies Hitler's Aryan ideal, and reflects the insidious propaganda behind recruiting the young German into the Hitler Youth movement. While claiming that the future of Germany lay in the hands of the young, Hitler used the 'Youth' as an easily manipulated and willing body to promote his own ideals.

Rallies (such as the one at Dresden, entitled 'Germany Awake!' right), did much to restore national pride and promote a new sense of self respect in a nation ravaged and humiliated after World War 1.

Hitler had his imitators in other parts of Europe. In Britain, Baronet Sir Oswald Mosley (left) though of very different background from the little Austrian corporal, had much in common with him politically. Mosley and his supporters adopted the uniform, salute, moustache and rhetoric of Hitler's Fascism. Seen left at the largest Fascist Rally held in Britain, in October 1936, Mosley headed a march of 10,000 men and women through South-East London.

Hitler's admiration of Benito Mussolini, the Italian Fascist leader, amounted to hero-worship: their joint intention was to subject all Europe to Fascism. Pictured right, at Munich, they met to discuss the terms of French capitulation.

58

But the extent of Nazi hostility towards Jews (as well as other 'undesirables' such as gypsies, Jehovah's Witnesses, homosexuals and the mentally ill) has few parallels. Persecution was systematized once the Nazis were firmly in power. The Nuremburg Laws of 1935, passed by Hitler, explicitly denied German citizenship to Jews, forbad their professional activity, and banned marriage or sexual liaison betwen Jews and 'nationals of German or similar blood'.

The brutal effects of these laws were the subject of a poem by Bertolt Brecht called *The Ballad of Marie Sanders*. Marie has a Jewish lover. Friends warn her about the new laws but she ignores their advice. She is arrested and suffers public humiliation:

One morning, close on nine,
She was driven through the town
In her slip, round her neck a sign,
*   her hair all shaven.*
The street was yelling. She
coldly stared.

The Jewish tragedy developed in earnest in 1938, when a Polish Jew killed a German official in Paris. It was an excuse for an orgy of anti-Jewish violence throughout Germany, which became known as the *Kristallnacht* (Crystal Night) because of all the glass from the broken windows of Jewish shopkeepers that lay in the street the next day.

Attacks on Jews were followed by simultaneous outbreaks of fire in nine of the 12 synagogues in Berlin. Gangs of youths roamed the street, smashing the windows of any Jewish shop they came across. They were dressed in plain clothes, but seemed to be working to a plan – the Nazi plan – and their rampage continued unchecked. A *London Times* correspondent wrote 'During the entire day hardly a policeman was to be seen in the streets where the 'purge' was in progress, save those for directing traffic'.

In Germany as a whole, at least 7,000 Jewish shops were pillaged, 36 Jews killed and over 20,000 arrested. Official reaction to the pogrom was predictable: a blind eye was turned towards the instigators, while the victims were fined a total of over a billion marks.

In 1933 Germany had a Jewish population of over half a million. By 1939 more than 50 per cent had escaped or emigrated, and those remaining were interned in the first concentration camps. The idea of a 'final solution to the Jewish question' was eventually agreed upon by leading Nazis in 1942. Fourteen million Jews throughout Europe, including Britain, were listed for annihilation.

Had Hitler restricted himself to a policy of 'race purity' within Germany, he might well have achieved it, unquestioned by neighbours anxious to avoid war. But his goal was to establish German supremacy over all Europe, and also to eradicate all Jews, Communists and dissenters from a German Europe. He gambled that no-one would dare to gainsay him. It took World War II to prove him wrong and to scotch his ambitions.

Hitler's Imitators
In the 1920s, Hitler had been inspired by the Italian Fascist Benito Mussolini. By the thirties, Hitler, too, became an inspiration for a new generation of right-wing extremists: in fact his success overshadowed his Italian hero.

Imitators sought to develop Fascist parties in other countries, including Hungary, France and Britain.

They all combined nationalism, anti-Communism, a distrust of democracy, and an emphasis on the single-party state, ruled by a charismatic leader. Virulent anti-Semitism was probably the main distinction between Hitler and Mussolini. Even in Italy, however, anti-Jewish legislation was passed in 1938, in response to German pressure.

The British Union of Fascists was formed by Oswald Mosley in 1932. The blackshirt uniform was borrowed from Mussolini, but the anti-Semitism came from Hitler. Mosley held provocative marches and rallies, especially in the Jewish quarters of London's East End. In the 'Battle of Cable Street' in 1936, anti-Fascist demonstrators, Blackshirts and police clashed. Mosley was obliged to call off the march. He was furious, claiming that the British government had finally given in to communism.

Mainly as a response to Mosley's provocations, the Public Order Act (1936) banned political uniforms and private armies. It contributed to the decline of the British Union of Fascists.

Recently Mosley's son was asked for his views on his father's political activities in the thirties. His reply captures the ambiguity within all Fascist movements:

While the right hand dealt with grandiose ideas and glory, the left hand let the rat out of the sewer.

The logical conclusion of Hitler's actions was war. Recruitment posters (below) urged the support of the nation by enlisting in the Reichswehr – the 100,000-man army that would unite all the German-speaking peoples within one empire. This was Hitler's dream, but destiny was to see it fail in the cataclysm of World War II.

MacClancy Collection

THE GREAT COMPOSERS

Gustav Holst

1874–1934

Gustav Holst was inspired by the folk songs and church music of his native England, yet his was not a purely nationalist style; he brought to his compositions a cosmopolitan flavour unique to English music of his time. His influence as a music teacher was perhaps equally profound. He sought to both challenge and encourage his students to reach his own high musical standards. Holst used his interest in astrology to provide a starting point for his best-known composition, The Planets, analysed in the Listener's Guide; *however, he shunned the fame its great success brought to him. He was not tempted simply to repeat himself, but continued to grow and diversify as a composer. In his teaching post at St. Paul's Girls' School, Holst was a strong advocate of educational equality for women;* In The Background *describes the struggle of women in Britain to earn equal social and political status.*

Gustav Holst showed oustanding musical promise as a child; his father, a virtuoso musician, hoped Holst would become a concert pianist. Yet Holst, knowing that his poor physical health made him unsuited to such a career, yearned to compose; he began to do so in secret. He won a scholarship to the Royal College of Music on his second attempt. After college, he played trombone in bands and orchestras before becoming a music teacher. Holst was revolutionary as a teacher, shunning traditional methods and demanding the best of his students. He set equally high standards for his own compositions, writing challenging works based on English folk songs, contemporary literature and Hindu poetry. His first success came with The Planets in 1918. But success made him uneasy; with his introspective nature and poor health, he wanted only to live and work quietly. Despite physical pain, he held his teaching posts and composed prolifically until his death in 1934.

'A "real composer"'

Gustav Holst produced one of this century's most popular works with the magnificent Planets. But fame and acclaim rested uneasily on the shoulders of this shy, retiring composer.

Adolphus Holst (right), pianist, organist and conductor, settled in Cheltenham (far right) in the 1890s. He married one of his pupils, Clara Lediard (above), and their first child, Gustav, was born in September 1874.

Gustav Holst was born on 21 September 1874 in a small Regency house in Cheltenham, Gloucestershire, England. He was named after his grandfather, a harpist and music teacher who had settled in Cheltenham in the 1840s. Holst's father, Adolphus, continued the musical traditions of the family – he was an excellent all-round musician. He gave piano lessons, played the organ on Sundays in a local church and gave recitals. In due course he married one of his pupils, a solicitor's daughter, Clara Lediard, and Gustav was their first child.

Gustav and his brother Emil (he later became an actor known as Ernest Cossart) found their father, the sound of whose virtuoso playing was a constant part of their childhood, to be an exacting teacher. When their hands were large enough to tackle 'five-finger exercises' they began music lessons and practised with him daily. He was held in great regard by his pupils and audiences but at home he was not really a family man. His grand-daughter, Imogen Holst, related that the family found him 'an uncomfortable man to live with'.

Gustav was a delicate child – short-sighted and prone to asthma and, although naturally boisterous, was not at all strong. His prediliction for indoor pursuits like reading and music is therefore not surprising. When he was eight his mother died and a few years later his father remarried another of his pupils, whose main interest was theosophy. Holst's own interest in religious philosophy developed later, although he might have heard many interesting discussions from his step-mother's friends.

From the age of 12 Holst began to try his hand at composition. Unfortunately his activities in this direction were hindered, rather than helped, by his father who discouraged composition and banned the music of Holst's favourite composer, Grieg, from the house. Holst had to continue his attempts – his 'early horrors', as he called them – in secret, late at night, and he could only air them on the piano when his father was out of the house. He learned his first principles of composition from his reading of Berlioz's *Treatise on Modern Instrumentation and Orchestration,* and from the practical experience he gained later conducting small choirs.

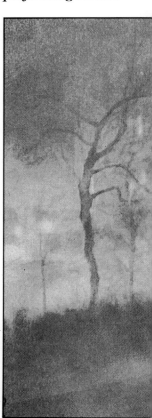

Holst (left) showed great musical promise early on and his father hoped he would become a concert pianist. Holst, however, became more interested in composition. He was a frail child, though, and before long his father realized that he just did not have the constitution for a performing career.

Unenthusiastic about his son's interest in composition, Adolph Holst did however nurture great hopes that Gustav might have a future as a concert pianist. Although Holst showed great promise from an early age he suffered increasingly from neuritis in his right arm and eventually his father had to face the fact that he would never be fit enough for a career as a virtuoso performer.

His first professional appointment after he left school, aged 17, was as organist and choirmaster, on pay of £4 per annum, to the village parish of Wyck Rissington, near Cheltenham. The following year he was invited to conduct the Choral Society of a neighbouring village, Bourton-on-the-Water. Once his father had realized that he would not be able to pursue a career as a performer he gave permission for his son to attend a two-month course in harmony and counterpoint in Oxford. After this it was decided that he would go to London to study composition at the Royal College of Music.

A student in London

Holst arrived in London in May 1893 and began life as a student at the Royal College of Music. At first he felt depressed since he had failed to win an open scholarship for composition and did not relish the fact that his father was paying his fees. Also his teacher of Composition, Stanford, was not always complimentary about his work. He corrected it heavily and constantly told Holst: 'It won't do, me boy'. However, in 1895 Holst was successful in winning a scholarship for composition thereby achieving financial independence from his father and acceptance as a serious composer.

During 1895 Holst met a fellow-student, Ralph Vaughan Williams. Vaughan Williams, himself destined to be a famous composer, became Holst's greatest musical confidant and lifelong friend. Later Holst recalled their student days when they sought each other out for mutual advice on their work:

What one really learns from college is not so much from one's official teachers as from one's fellow students. We used to meet at a little tea-shop in Kensington and discuss every subject from the lowest note of the bassoon to the philosophy of Thomas Hardy's 'Jude the Obscure'.

His second instrument at college was the trombone. Not only did learning this instrument help to cure his asthma but it also gave him an insight into orchestration from the viewpoint of the player. It also provided him with a means of income, as he played professionally in pier orchestras during his vacations, and in London theatres in winter.

The style of work which he showed to Vaughan Williams owed much to the music of Wagner – tickets for the standing room in the gallery of Covent Garden on Wagner nights were high on his list of priorities and soon after his arrival in London he had heard the Ring cycle. He was entranced by the startling new sounds, quite unlike anything he had heard before.

During these stimulating student days Holst was introduced to the work of contemporary poets such as George Meredith, Francis Thompson and Robert Bridges, and settings of some of their poems are found in his early works. Bridges, who became a great friend of Holst's, was the future poet laureate. Other writers whose work greatly influenced Holst's thinking and creativity were Walt Whitman, the American poet, and William Morris, artist, designer and socialist writer. It was after reading some of Morris's essays on Socialism that Holst decided to join the Hammersmith Socialist Club which met at Kelmscott House, Morris's Thameside home.

As it happened, the newly-formed Hammersmith Socialist Choir needed a conductor and Holst soon found himself in charge. In the course of rehearsals Holst met and fell in love with one of the sopranos,

Holst went to study composition at the Royal College of Music in London in 1893. He found student life there invigorating and made many strong friendships. One of these was with Ralph Vaughan Williams (below), who was later to become a famous composer.

Like most students Holst found that he needed extra money, and so he took to playing trombone (his second instrument) professionally. In summer he played in pier orchestras at the seaside and in the winter pantomime season he played in theatre orchestras in Leicester Square (below left).

Holst Birthplace Museum

Holst Birthplace Museum

In 1901 Holst married Isobel Harrison. They were unable to afford a honeymoon then, but in 1903 holidayed in Berlin (left). Their only child, Imogen (above), was born in 1907.

for his development as a creative artist there was little money to be made out of the publication of isolated short works, and for a while had to exist on what Isobel could earn as a dressmaker.

Music maker

Deliverance came in the form of a part-time teaching position at James Allens Girls' School in Dulwich. He gratefully accepted and made such a success of the job that he was invited to stay permanently. Two years later he took up the post of Director of Music at St Paul's Girls' School, Hammersmith, an appointment that he held until the end of his life. Many of his compositions were dedicated to the school: the most famous of the 'St Paul's' compositions – a piece for strings called *St Paul's Suite,* 1913, is not only one of Holst's finest works but also a testament to the high standard of the school orchestra.

Teaching was in Holst's blood and he took it very seriously and for his time was revolutionary in his methods. He hated harmony textbooks and compulsory examinations. He always believed in giving his pupils music that he was particularly fond of himself and not what he called 'the reams of twaddle' sent to him by publishers as 'suitable for girls'.

In keeping with the socialist ideal that art and

Isobel Harrison. He thought her the most enchanting girl he had ever met, and although it took some time to convince her of his own charms, he eventually persuaded her to marry him. At this stage he was about to leave college and it was clear to both of them that it would be some time before they could get married.

An oriental outlook

After leaving college he became interested in Indian literature, and was captivated by the rich poetry of the ancient texts of the Hindu *Rig Veda,* which he read in translation. He set some passages from this to music – enrolling at the London School of Oriental Languages, so that he could learn enough Sanskrit to make his own translations. His lessons there, from Dr Mabel Bode, made a lasting impression on him and he adopted certain oriental beliefs in his own outlook on life.

To finance himself after leaving college in 1898 Holst took up the trombone in a more serious way. He joined the Carl Rosa Opera Company as principal trombone and rehearsal pianist, and later did some touring with the Scottish Orchestra. In London he occasionally worked in the White Viennese Band. Members of the Band had to dress in a white and gold uniform and were under strict orders to put on Austrian accents for the benefit of the audience!

In 1901 he and Isobel were married and set up home in a couple of furnished rooms above a shop in Shepherds Bush. They could not afford a honeymoon, but in 1903 with the help of a legacy from his father's estate, Holst and Isobel decided to take a holiday in Germany. They stayed with Holst's second cousin, Mathias, in Berlin and were introduced to the concert life of the city and to a large circle of musicians and music lovers. Holst was amazed by the passion Germans had for new music.

When he returned to England Holst gave up his trombone-playing career and decided to turn his attentions to serious work as a composer. In any case, life as a touring musician had been tiring and had left him no time for composing. Although it was better

S. Kay 'Barnes Terrace'. Courtesy of the Paton Collection

education should be available to everybody irrespective of income, Holst began teaching evening classes in 1907 at Morley College — an adult education centre for working-class people. Among Holst's students were cab-drivers, tram conductors, policemen, ladies' maids and even a cricket bat maker! The Morley College orchestra began life with two violins, one flute, three clarinets, all at the sharp pitch, a cornet and a piano. But before long they had improved their resources and standards enough to be able to give the first performance since 1697 of Purcell's masque, *The Fairy Queen.*

Teaching had brought employment, enjoyment and relative prosperity into Holst's life. Just after their daughter Imogen was born in 1907 the Holsts could afford to rent an elegant terraced house in Barnes, overlooking the river, and they moved there in 1908. Now Holst's only problem was that such a punishing teaching schedule left very little time for composition. Only on Sundays and during the school holidays could he manage to escape to the large airy music room at the top of the house where he could work in perfect peace. But he rarely complained about his teaching responsibilities and often declared that writing music for his pupils to sing meant a great deal to him.

A luke-warm reception

Out of school Holst's works fared less well. Few people were prepared to put money into new music at the time and Holst frequently became discouraged. The first piece to be composed in his new music room was inspired by Sanskrit literature — the opera *Savitri,* based on the old legends of the Mahabharata. Although it was the first chamber opera to be composed in England since Purcell's day it did not have a performance until eight years later. Another 'Indian' work, *The Cloud Messenger,* was given a performance in 1913, but it was poorly received. In the spring of 1913, the sponsor of the concert where *The Cloud Messenger* was performed, the composer Balfour Gardiner, rescued Holst from his misery with the invitation to a holiday in Spain with his friends, the brothers Arnold and Clifford Bax. On this holiday he was to find the enthusiasm to write a large orchestral work — *The Planets* — which was to become his best known work.

Music at Thaxted

From 1913 the Essex town of Thaxted became the scene of family life for the Holsts. When not at work composing, Holst spent his time taking long walks, or music making at the local church. He spent much effort on the little choir, which was already rather good at plainchant and which, with encouragement from Holst, soon learnt to give passable performances of music by Byrd and other 16th-century English composers. One day it occurred to Holst that it would be a splendid idea to import the Morley and St Paul's Choirs to Thaxted for an informal festival of early music. The first Festival was arranged for Whitsun 1916, and was a huge success.

Everyone who took part in or attended the

Before he became established as a composer, Holst became music master at St Paul's Girls' School, Hammersmith, a post which he held until the end of his life. In the sketch above he is shown conducting a section of the school orchestra. Teaching brought relative prosperity to Holst and in 1908 the family moved to No 10, The Terrace, Barnes (left — their house second from right).

Holst was found unfit for combat but, in 1918, was sent to Salonika (shown in the postcard above, which he sent to his wife) as music master for the YMCA's army education scheme

The sketch above (featuring Holst, batted and conducting), captures the busy atmosphere of amateur music-making at the Whitsun Festivals. Holst initiated annual festivals of music at the Essex village of Thaxted, where he lived after 1914. Later, these were held in St Albans, Canterbury and Chichester.

Thaxted Festival felt it was worth repeating, and so, for the following two years, the forces regathered to sing at Whitsuntide. Holst wrote music especially for the Thaxted combined choir and one of the pieces is the now famous carol *This have I done for my true love.*

There was no festival in 1919 as Holst was posted abroad. Although not fit for combat himself, he was sent to do educational work among the troops who were about to be demobilized. In the autumn of 1918 he was posted to Constantinople and Salonika as Musical organizer for the YMCA army education scheme.

Holst returned home to England in the summer of 1919 and went back to his accustomed routine of teaching all week and composing on Sundays. Public interest in his music was now stirring and there were more opportunities for performances of his works. In March 1920 he had a memorable performance of his choral work *Hymn of Jesus* and a few months later came the first complete public performance under his own baton of *The Planets.*

It did not take him long to discover the disadvantages of fame. He was an unworldly man with no idea how to handle either the press or admirers and was often accused of looking sullen when taking a bow. His chief objection to all the attention was the potential danger he felt it represented to his art. He wrote to his friend Clifford Bax, 'Some day I expect you will agree with me that it's a great thing to be a failure. If nobody likes your work you have to go on for the sake of the work. And you are in no danger of

letting the public make you repeat yourself. Every artist ought to pray that he may not be a success.'

During the early years of the 1920s up to 1923, Holst's popularity was at its peak. Performances of his work conducted by himself were invariably sold out. Apart from his performing engagements, his teaching commitments had also increased. He was professor at the Royal College of Music and was appointed to the staff of University College Reading. It was at Reading in February 1923 while conducting the student orchestra that an accident occurred which was to result in serious illness. He fell backwards off the podium and was concussed. He appeared to recover very quickly and his doctor allowed him to go ahead with plans to travel to America on a lecturing tour. However, not long after his return to England he began to suffer from sleeplessness and pains in the head which were probably the delayed effects of the concussion.

A complete rest was prescribed, so he cancelled all engagements for 1924 and retired to Thaxted, where, in the words of a letter he wrote to a friend he felt he led 'the combined lives of Real Composer and Tame Cat!'

Return to London

At the beginning of 1925 Holst was allowed back to London life and a limited resumption of his teaching activities. Outwardly he appeared in good health, but it was to be a long while before he could tolerate traffic noise or crowds. Although he was only 50 years old he seemed older – his hair was almost completely white, and he had lost the usual spring in his step. Craftily, though, he used his discomfort to his best advantage – as an excuse to miss the social functions which he found tedious.

One benefit, though, was that he found more time to enjoy the company of close friends. Ralph Vaughan Williams, still his closest friend, was a constant companion although musically they seemed to be growing apart.

Another friend was the novelist Thomas Hardy, whose novels and poetry had appealed to Holst in his student days. In the 1920s, after setting some of Hardy's poems as songs, Holst sent the works to the poet. Hardy received them warmly and over the ensuing years their friendship grew. Hardy was to provide Holst with the subject of his orchestral work, *Egdon Heath.* Holst felt the work grew out of a sentence in Hardy's novel *The Return of the Native.* In it the heath is described as 'A place perfectly accordant with Man's nature – neither ghastly, hateful nor ugly; neither commonplace, unmeaning nor tame, but like Man, slighted and enduring, and, withal, singularly colossal and mysterious in its swarthy monotony.'

The work was performed in Cheltenham Town Hall where it was well-received, but the first London performance was disastrous. Holst, however, was not discouraged, for although his popularity had declined since its peak in 1923, he knew he was producing better music than ever.

Holst Birthplace Museum

One of Holst's most important works after the **The Planets** *was* **Egdon Heath,** *which he dedicated to* **Thomas Hardy (left).** *According to Holst (shown above in the last photograph taken of him),* **Egdon Heath** *grew out of a sentence in Hardy's novel* **The Return of the Native** *and he personally considered it his best piece of music.*

H. G. Eves 'Thomas Hardy' The National Portrait Gallery, London

During the next five years he was very productive. Works from these years include the opera *The Wandering Scholar,* the *Double Concerto* for two violins, the *Choral Fantasia,* written for the three Choir Festival, *Hammersmith,* a tone poem full of the sounds and sights of riverside London, and the *Lyric Movement* for viola and small orchestra. They all add up to what is possibly the finest testimony to creativity that he could have had in his last years.

In 1932 Holst spent six months enjoying the great honour of being guest lecturer at Harvard University. This gave him the opportunity to conduct highly successful performances of his music with the Boston Symphony Orchestra. Unfortunately, just before leaving Harvard for a tour of Canada he fell ill with a stomach complaint caused either by a duodenal or gastric ulcer. He had to spend several weeks convalescing but was well enough to attend a concert of his work given as a tribute by the University.

Back in England Holst seemed to be making a full recovery, but in early 1933 he suffered a relapse and from then on spent most of his time in and out of hospitals. Throughout 1934, the last year of his life, despite constant pain, he managed to keep cheerful and, although with great difficulty, managed to go on writing music until the end.

He died on 25 May 1934, and at the request of one of his friends, Bishop Bell, his ashes were buried in the north aisle of Chichester Cathedral. As a tribute to him the choir sang his lovely Thaxted carol, 'This have I done for my true love.'

The Planets

In this, his best known and most popular work, Holst presents a series of evocative musical portraits based on the individual 'characters' of seven planets.

The Planets was Holst's first large scale composition and has become the work for which he is most remembered. For Holst, the extent of his success with the work was unexpected, especially as it came after a period of failure and disillusionment.

In the spring of 1913, Holst went on holiday to Majorca, a trip which was a precious escape for him as he had just had a depressing failure with *The Cloud Messenger* which had flopped before a first-night audience in London. The performance was part of a series of concerts featuring new music by young British composers, organized by Balfour Gardiner, a composer and wealthy promoter of contemporary artists. Gardiner liked to use his wealth to further the cause of new music and was well known for his generosity, so while the despondent Holst declared himself to be 'fed up with music, especially my own,' it was Gardiner who took him off to Majorca in an attempt to raise his spirits.

In Majorca, the seeds of *The Planets* were sown. The holiday was a great success — Gardiner and Holst were joined by another composer, Arnold Bax, and his brother Clifford, an author. Not only were Holst's spirits uplifted by the beauty of the island, but he was able to relax in the most agreeable company and embark on endless discussions about the intricacies of orchestration with the other two composers. But perhaps the most significant feature of the trip was that it led to a deepening of Holst's fascination with astrology after finding he shared an interest in the subject with Clifford Bax. For his own amusement, Holst liked to cast his friends' horoscopes, playfully calling it his 'pet vice', but after his discussions with the knowledgeable Clifford Bax, he began to study this subject more closely.

There was always a close relationship between Holst's musical composition and his extra-musical intellectual pursuits. Indeed, they were often a direct source of inspiration for him. Earlier in his career he had become interested in Indian philosophy and literature and even taught himself Sanskrit in order to make his own translations. This led to his composition of a number of pieces of Eastern inspiration. Through astrology Holst found that each planet was attributed with a very individual character, and it was his resolve to interpret these characters musically which provided the framework for his large-scale orchestral suite.

Holst began composing *Mars,* the first of the movements, in 1914 before the outbreak of war, so the piece was really a prophecy of, not a reaction to, World War I which was to follow. The last piece to be written was *Mercury* and Holst finished orchestrating the whole suite only in 1916, fitting in time for composition between his teaching duties at St. Paul's Girls' school in London. Because of the neuritis in his right arm, much of the 200 page orchestral score had to be dictated to his colleagues on the music staff at St Paul's, Nora Day and Vally Lasker, whom he affectionately called his 'scribes'. Holst put the score away in a drawer when it was finished, convinced that no-one would be able to afford to produce the work during wartime as it demanded such a large orchestra.

Once again it was Balfour Gardiner who gave Holst the support he needed in providing the means for the new work to be heard. He hired the Queen's Hall and its orchestra for a semi-private performance in September 1918, which was conducted by a young man who in Holst's phrase 'first made *The Planets* shine' — the 29-year-old Adrian Boult.

Boult had only two hours to rehearse this very difficult music from the hastily scribbled parts, but the composer's daughter Imogen described this première performance as 'in some ways the best of all'. She recalled:

The two or three hundred friends or fellow musicians who had come to listen in the half-dark auditorium realized that

The inspiration for The Planets *stemmed from Holst's interest in astrology. The zodiacal signs (right) are characterized by the planets which influence them. And it was Holst's idea to interpret the planets' individual characters in music which provides the framework for his orchestral suite.*

THE PLANETS
by
GUSTAV HOLST.

MARS, the bringer of war. VENUS, the bringer of peace. MERCURY, the winged messenger. JUPITER, the bringer of jollity. SATURN, the bringer of old age. URANUS, the magician. NEPTUNE, the mystic.

Goodwin & Tabb LTD.   Full Orchestral Score.

By permission of the British Library

Holst completed the score of The Planets *(title page left) in 1916, but with Britain still at war he held no hope of finding funds for the large orchestra required to perform it. In fact, it was not until his friend and fellow composer, Balfour Gardiner generously offered financial support, in 1918, that the work was premièred in London.*

Ptolemeus Aegyptius

Azophi Arabus

Antoine Wiertz 'Un Grand de la Terre'. Musees royaux de Belgique, Bruxelles

played but reaction to *The Planets* was rapturous – so different to that received in 1913 after the performance of the doomed *Cloud Messenger*. The work continued to be popular and has, in spite of Holst's bewilderment, ensured his lasting fame.

Programme notes

Mars, the Bringer of War

Mars opens with a simple tapped rhythm on timpani and violin (*col legno*, using the wooden backs of the bows). Over this the bassoons and horns play a slow, and menacing three-note phrase that struggles up from G to D and sinks back to D flat, before rising to a sharp crescendo on the gong. This is repeated several times, the growling brass rising and falling with inexorable persistence. The three-note phrase of the horns reaches higher in an attempt to ennoble the piece but the effort is quashed. The trumpets rear clamorously infusing the music with a sense of panic. The opening rhythm quickens as it is thundered out heavily on the brass. After three bars of this brutal intensity, a new theme enters through the trombones and then horns. But there is still no respite in the rhythm until the strings climb into their higher register and, with blocked chords, enforce a new metre. The trombone now lends its weight to the strings' mechanical repetition, by playing a new tune which is attended by little trumpet fanfares. The violins extend the new theme triumphantly then the trumpet and tenor

J. B. Pierre 'Baccanale'. Musee Crozatier, Le Puy-en-Velay/Lauros-Giraudon

The brutal character of 'Mars', fiery and bitterly destructive, is the subject of Holst's opening movement of the Planets. His rendition of 'the bringer of war', must have been all the more spine-chilling for the first audiences, who had the horrors of World War I still fresh in mind.

this was no ordinary occasion: the music was quite unlike anything they had heard before. They found the clamour of Mars almost unbearable after four years of a war that was still going on. During Jupiter *the charwomen working in the corridors put down their scrubbing-brushes and began to dance. In Saturn the middle-aged listeners felt themselves growing older with every bar. But it was the end of Neptune that was unforgettable, with its hidden chorus of women's voices growing fainter and fainter in the distance, until the imagination knew no difference between sound and silence.*

The first public performance was given a few weeks later while Holst was abroad. Only five of the seven movements were

'Jupiter', the fourth movement is 'the bringer of jollity', whose playful, carefree nature is echoed in the bacchanalian scene, right. Some early performances of The Planets were made without the last three movements, much to Holst's annoyance, finishing with 'Jupiter' to give the work a happier ending.

tuba pursue each other with a shrieking five-note motif which reaches ever higher, until finally the horns protest. The winds and strings scurry away and the music plunges on to a massive sustained chord. But immediately the horror is resumed, as the lower strings and the bassoons reiterate the insidious line of two-note groups earlier played by trombones and horns, while the sidedrum's quiet 5/4 rhythm implies the sound of distant gunfire. A crescendo brings the gunfire closer as the canker of the insidious phrase spreads through all the instruments. Once more every member of the vast orchestra blasts out the 5/4 rhythm. The opening G, D, D-flat motif returns with renewed force and the relentless pounding of the drums pervades as other earlier phrases are recalled with increased ferocity. A howling discord seems to protest against the inhuman turmoil and is echoed by the strings before the music is dissipated by the final cruel hammer-blows. But there is no compromise in the ultimate chord with its thundering low register quadruple *forte* (strong, loud).

Venus, the Bringer of Peace

Holst quickly banishes the angry mood of *Mars* with just four rising notes of the solo horn, suggesting an utterly different terrain of space, light and tranquillity. Cool flutes descend in reply, and chords in horns, flutes and harps sway consolingly back and forth. The swaying chords expire in the upper air (flute chord); the solo

Understanding music: teaching music

Music has always been part of the education of civilized society and the possession of musical skills and the appreciation of musical art has long been held a sign of an educated person. Equally venerable is the tradition which regards music as physically and mentally beneficial – even as a moral force.

Music was a central part of Plato's educational system precisely for this reason: 'The absence of grace, rhythm and harmony is closely related to baseness of character, whereas their presence goes with moral excellence and self-mastery.'

The Church took the same view, and in the Middle Ages, the monasteries and cathedral schools developed instruction in singing and produced the first musical treatises. The first chair in music at a university was established at Salamanca in 1254 and music lectures were given in many universities from this period. By the end of the medieval period, separate music faculties were established at Oxford and Cambridge; while the minstrel tradition of courtly love, which required a chivalrous lover to compose and perform his own love songs, made music a necessary aristocratic accomplishment.

The Renaissance, which revived classical learning in many fields, emphasized the humanistic aspect of music and the 'Renaissance man' was expected to be accomplished in many spheres, music among them. The first music tutors were published as printing developed, which freed both the spread of musical works and musical instruction from dependence upon personal contact. Church, school and music were closely linked during the Reformation in Protestant Germany, and Martin Luther once said, 'A schoolmaster must know how to sing or I will not allow him to teach.' In the 17th and 18th centuries, the two main influences were the increasing importance of secular music (especially opera), and the growth of the middle class. In Germany and the Low Countries, the guilds took on the role of music educators, while in Italy, the first establishments devoted entirely to music-teaching – the conservatories – grew up, and subsequently spread to Germany and France. Composition-teaching was becoming more standardized, and that most famous of tutors, the *Gradus ad Parnassum* of J. J. Fux was published in 1725.

In England, many of these developments were delayed until the 19th century, partly because of the anti-musical (more precisely, anti-theatrical) Puritan heritage and partly because of the low standard of education generally. English musicians were often trained in Germany, at least until the founding of the Royal College of Music in 1883. After this late start, England took a lead in making good music more widely available via inexpensive concert series such as the Henry Wood 'Proms' (inaugurated in 1895) and through broadcasting. The original motives of the British Broadcasting Corporation, founded in 1922, were not dissimilar from those of Plato, and the BBC included from the outset music lessons in its educational broadcasts. Also in the 1920s, Robert Mayer began his children's concerts and Ernest Read his varied activities in music education.

Elsewhere, this century has seen the development of several systems of music education. In Hungary, the method devised by Zoltán Kodály (1882–1967) emphasized the importance of teaching children sight-singing, while in Germany, Orff's school, which explored the relationship between music and movement, also had great influence on the use of music in elementary education throughout the world. In Japan, Shin'ichi Suzuki (b.1898) invented his method of teaching the violin to large classes of very young children, and today, there are many professional concert artists trained by the Suzuki method. In the West, performers are still usually trained by other famous performers, which sustains traditions and provides a pedigree – as the pianist, Claudio Arrau says, 'I was a pupil of Krause, who was a pupil of Liszt, who was a pupil of Czerny, who was a pupil of Beethoven!'

Music teaching is an activity which many composers have also undertaken. Schütz was taught by Giovanni Gabrieli, Beethoven by Haydn (not very well), Stravinsky by Rimsky-Korsakov, Vaughan Williams by Ravel, Britten by Frank Bridge, Boulez by Messiaen. Probably the most influential of 20th-century teachers was Schoenberg, who taught Berg and Webern directly and many others through his theories and writings. In England, composers have contributed much to school music, either by teaching in schools as Holst did, or by writing music for performance by schoolchildren, such as Britten's *Noye's Fludde*.

The 20th century has seen a split between professional and amateur music-making which is reflected in the musical appreciation movement. This movement, which takes many forms, aims to bring to people the masterpieces of music, though classes, talks, gramophone societies and publications.

horn rises, and the flutes descend, once again. A sustained high note in strings and flutes and a little vigour from a solo cello lead us to a shining woodwind chord from which a solo violin emerges, singing a tune whose sweetness is pure balm:

Example 1

♪ *solo violin*
p

All the violins repeat and extend the melody, with the many two-note falling phrases sounding like great sighs of contentment. As the solo violin returns, an oboe adds an expressive arching phrase. The full body of the strings repeat the oboe phrase with even more passion and a solo cello gives one last caress to it as it passes.

The swaying chords return, their gentle oscillation evoking a sublime atmosphere of peace and tranquillity. The solo horn's four notes are heard again, and the muted violins play Example 1 for the last time with the solo cello once more languor-ously adding its caress. The flute's descent ushers in the coda of swaying horns and harps. Only now does the texture of this translucently scored movement become fuller. Finally, the tinkling of the celesta and a very high sustained note in the violins brings *Venus* to an ethereal close.

Mercury, the Winged Messenger
After the calm of *Venus, Mercury* is all restless activity. It opens with fragments of rapid quavers darting to and fro around the orchestra in kaleidoscopic shafts and flashes of instrumental colour. The light sounds of the harp and celesta, used throughout the *Planets* for their heavenly associations, emerge from the bustle to introduce the first 'tune.' This is then picked out in the oboe and English horn and given a fanfare-like tail by winds and strings. The tune lingers with various instrumental groups before a solo violin swells the melody into a free and airy mood. The whole orchestra then takes it up and swiftly builds it to a climax, the only *fortissimo* (very loud) in *Mercury*. With the descent from this climax comes the return of the restless opening music, into what Imogen Holst compared to the sound of 'buffeting currents of air' — the whole body of muted strings, pp and staccato, race across the score like the wind itself. There is a rush of energy as the woodwind joins in, in various combinations and with alternating loud and quiet passages. A sudden halt, a tense drumbeat, and the celesta brings back the tentative first tune,

Of all the movements of the **Planets** *'Saturn' was Holst's favourite. 'The Bringer of Old Age' is an evocation of the relentless passage of time, as symbolized in this painting (right) with the ancient god and his scythe – a grim reminder of death – presiding over Dawn's daily resurgence.*

its tail now on flute and piccolo. Then the solo violin returns to the second 'airy' melody, and celesta and harps briefly have the scene to themselves again. A flourish rises up through the whole woodwind family, culminating on a high sustained note on the violin. Double bassoon and double bass sound the tiny fanfare and, with the briefest of chords, the winged messenger is gone.

Jupiter, the Bringer of Jollity
Jupiter, like *Mercury,* bursts on to the scene with turbulence and bustle. Over the strings' fast figuration the horns, violas and cello play a syncopated tune with a rhythm reminiscent of early Stravinsky ballets. The theme is repeated at once, this time with an added coda. A horn fanfare is followed by the little coda phrase, then the trumpet and woodwind try the fanfare. This proves as infectious as laughter and more instruments take it up. A *ritenuto* (holding back of the tempo) prepares us for the second real tune in a movement filled with melody. The horns play a tune marked *molto pesante* (very heavily), with woodwind and glockenspiel following on. The syncopated opening theme returns and the trumpet fanfare leads us into the

next tune where the 2/4 rhythm gives way to 3/4 and the beats in each bar give the melody a heavy, emphatic quality. Once more the horns lead the way, the woodwind and then the trumpets take up the tune as the pace quickens and the texture fills out towards a powerful climax. As this dies away a fanfare is quietly dotted around the orchestra and seems to call every member to attention as if something important is about to happen. The tempo slows to andante, and the strings and horns embark on the best loved of all Holst's melodies. Imogen, who is rather hard on her father over *Jupiter,* particularly

disliked the effect of this section: 'It is impossible to prevent an aura of patriotism hovering over an audience at this moment . . . backs become visibly straighter'.

The climax to which the melody builds is denied its final cadence, for the scurrying fanfares are keen to get things under way again. After this solemnity, the music reverts to the three tunes heard just before, this time the bell-like sound of the glockenspiel and the smack of the tambourine enlivens the third tune in the sequence and brings the movement to its final climax. This leads to a dramatic

change of key and broadening of tempo as the winds, strings and harps swirl as if in an Impressionist seascape, and the patriotic melody can be distinguished again as if through the mist. But it fades away short-lived, as the final *presto* very quickly sweeps all solemnity aside.

Saturn, the Bringer of Old Age
Saturn was Holst's own favourite among the seven movements. Even Imogen writes 'this is Holst's own sort of music'. It was a long time before musicians and audiences realized its significance, but it is *Saturn* that most looks forward to the power and austerity that characterized Holst's later works.

'The Bringer of Old Age' opens appropriately *adagio* and *piano,* 'slow' and 'quietly', with flutes and harps marking the pace of Time's inexorable tread.

Example 2

A slow, deep double bass phrase (x) begins in the fourth bar (and is later to take on greater significance) suggesting the stealth of approaching old age. Violins and the bass oboe play the phrase in turn, blending into the muted horns. The trombones play a mournful lament and Time's tread is resumed in the flutes with timpani and plucked basses marking the off-beats. Winds, harps and brass bring the spectre of death ever closer and panic breaks out: bells, struck urgently and 'with metal striker', toll for the loss of youth. The whole orchestra takes up the quicker rhythm and now the double bass phrase of the beginning is heard again, this time at its most desolate. But as the bells recede the height of the tragic clamour passes and an exquisitely consoling coda has the harps chiming peacefully. The ominous sound of the double bass phrase (x) is gradually transformed by ever more serene repetitions in the strings. Finally, all panic and fear is dissipated giving way to a calm acceptance of the inevitable as the music fades away.

Uranus, the Magician
The magician announces himself at once with a derisive incantation of four long notes.

Example 3

Some clumsy sounding staccato bassoons describe an atmosphere of sorcery and then the inelegant dance goes on its way, with staccato trumpets and the xylophone

Mariano Rossi 'Dawn and Time'. Galleria Borghese, Rome/Giraudon

Discovered as late as 1846, the planet Neptune took its name from the mythical god of the sea (right). Holst's eerie and mystical movement expresses with the utmost beauty the remoteness and mystery of this relatively 'new' planet.

prominent, until it possesses the whole orchestra. Then the horns, even more rollicking than the bassoons, introduce a new tune, the repetitions get louder and the orchestration brasher. Eventually, this is halted by the protest of the tuba playing the same four notes as shown in Example 3. The timpani take advantage of the temporary respite to strike up a solo, and the high woodwind fall over one another in derision. But the two kettledrums are determined to show they too can create a melody and they lead a dance which is soon joined by brass and tambourine. A mad pursuit breaks out again with renewed force, the xylophone adding a manic touch. Just when the din becomes almost intolerable, an organ *glissando* (slide) sweeps everything away. The music is now suddenly quite still, the string harmonies suggesting a region far removed from all the preceding chaos of 'magic-gone-wrong'. The harp recalls Example 3 but now its power to threaten has evaporated. The tubas try, and fail, to reassert its former mood, and all the brass

follow suit. But the final note of Example 3 dissolves on a great discord and its echoes fade into the strings' tranquil satisfaction. The magical has made way for the mystical.

Neptune, the Mystic

Neptune is the most visionary of all the movements and is the pinnacle of Holst's orchestral Impressionism. A footnote in the score indicates that 'the orchestra is to play *sempre* pp (always very quiet) throughout' and Holst even added to this in his own copy, 'dead tone, except the clarinet after 5'. Imogen comments, 'this is not the dead hush of despair: it is the intense concentration of a prolonged gaze into infinity.'

Three low flutes open the movement and meander across a great void, coming to rest on an oboe and piccolo chord. The trombone chord which immediately follows is discordant and seems quite alien, but earthly harmony has no role in *Neptune* – here all sounds can co-exist since they carry no emotional charge. More winds and the harps build a

shimmering texture which has nothing of sensuality in it. The eerie sound of the celesta floats across the vast emptiness, remote and without warmth. All is vaporous and incorporeal, no themes give shape to the music, which seems to recede ever further outwards beyond the planets, the universe and the mind. Eventually we are aware of a subtle change. The strings hold a low note, oboes and English horn meander above it, and a distant women's chorus sustains a quiet high B. The wordless sound is non-human and even though the clarinet is marked *dolce* (sweet) and is not bound by the 'dead tone' prescribed by Holst, its wandering line cannot resemble an earthly melody. The voices cease, the violins take up the clarinet's line, followed by the chorus in counterpoint, until halted by a sudden chord. The harps and celesta return to bring the work to a close. Bass flute and clarinet descend, the washes of harp glissandi sweep on and as the mystic voices fade away into the distant realms of the universe, the music simply disappears.

Great interpreters

Zubin Mehta (conductor)

Mehta was born in Bombay in 1936, the son of musical parents; in fact his father founded the Bombay String Quartet and Symphony Orchestra, of which he was also conductor. Zubin showed early musical leanings, and learned both piano and violin as a boy. By his mid-teens, however, he wanted to conduct, and was soon leading his father's orchestra in rehearsals.

Though persuaded to study medicine for two years, he abandoned it at the first opportunity and took up a place at the Vienna Academy of Music in 1954, at the age of 18. He studied conducting, as well as playing double bass in the Vienna Philharmonic. Here, he was able to experience both Furtwängler and Karajan at first hand, and he developed a deep admiration for the techniques of the former in particular. In 1955 he won a competition in Liverpool which enabled him to conduct a few concerts with the Liverpool Philharmonic and work with its

conductor John Pritchard. Within a short time he was guesting with a great many orchestras around Europe and in the U.S.A. By 1961 he had conducted both the Vienna Philharmonic Orchestra and the Berlin Philharmonic; the youngest conductor to do so. He later became musical director for both the Los Angeles Philharmonic and the Montreal Symphony, remaining at Montreal for two years, and with the L.A. Phil. until 1978.

In 1978, Mehta finally moved on from the L.A. Philharmonic, succeeding Pierre Boulez with the New York Philharmonic. He has also had a long association, both in concert and on record, with the Israel Philharmonic, finally becoming, in 1977, its musical director. For a man whose heart is clearly with the world of Mahler, Strauss and Bruckner, it is surprising to note that some of his greatest triumphs on record have been his opera recordings such as Puccini's *Turandot* and *Tosca*. A frequent guest conductor with the VPO, he will surely continue to be a central musical figure as the century progresses.

FURTHER LISTENING

Savitri
Holst was intensely interested in Sanskrit philosophy, and wrote a series of works employing Eastern modes of thought. This one-act opera is the most successful of these early pieces, and is also the most individual. Holst wrote both libretto and music, and although there are occasional lapses in both, the listener is left with a moving, if uneven, experience to digest.

Egdon Heath
This, one of Holst's most consistently inspired pieces, is not meant to depict a place in nature, but more to express a mood – symbolized, for Holst, by Egdon Heath.

Hammersmith – Orchestral Suite
This two-movement descriptive piece evokes an affectionate and accurate picture of this Thameside London suburb well known to the composer.

IN THE BACKGROUND

'Votes for women'

Holst's ancestral homeland, Sweden, was among the first European countries to enfranchize its womenfolk. In Britain, only a long struggle earned women the vote and their rightful social status.

Eyre Crowe 'The Dinner Hour, Wigan'. City of Manchester Art Gallery

From time immemorial to the late 19th century, most women had little or no say in the society in which they lived, and none had the right to vote. But with the arrival of industrialization large numbers of working women were brought together for the first time (left), marking the beginning of their development as a social force.

Holman Hunt's Awakening Conscience *(right) says much about the prevailing 19th-century attitudes to women – attitudes which long delayed women's suffrage. Full of symbolism, the picture preaches a visual sermon on the morality of the man and mistress relationship, via the woman's awakening to the dangers and vulnerability of her position. The picture thus exposes the hypocrisy of a society which condemns such a woman to ruin and shame while her seducer escapes without reproach.*

A cartoon (right) in the magazine Punch *speculated, in 1852, on the social repercussions of English women adopting the American 'habit' of bloomers. Its tone is derisive, and for many years derision was the only weapon men needed to quash women's emancipation.*

Women's rights – social equality and the right to vote (suffrage) – were advocated well over 2000 years ago by the Greek philosopher Plato. But women the world over had a long wait, in many cases until the early years of the 20th century, to find a place in society on an equal par with men. Even when the right to vote was granted it was most often after a long struggle on their part – women's right to vote was won rather than freely given. And nowhere was the battle for women's rights harder or longer fought than in Britain, where the suffragette movement campaigned for 25 years before seeing their dream of votes for all women realized.

The struggle for votes was generally just part of a wider movement towards the re-appraisal of

women's place in society. And this movement had its roots at least 100 years deep in history.

When Mary Wollstonecraft wrote *The Vindication of the Rights of Woman,* in 1792, she was mocked by Horace Walpole (novelist, member of Parliament and arbiter of public taste) as a 'hyena in petticoats'. There were then a great many things women lacked besides the vote: they could not receive a University education or become doctors; until 1870, a married woman could not own property; nor did she have the right to divorce her husband in the event of his adultery. These were more pressing injustices than the lack of a vote. After all, only one out of ten men had the vote themselves.

In Britain the issue of votes for women was first

seriously proposed by the philosopher John Stuart Mill in the 1860s, but elsewhere women were making practical strides. In America, they were attracted to the campaign to abolish slavery, and to the powerful temperance movement. In Wyoming, on the American frontier, women were given the vote as equals; and in Sweden, women were enfranchized for Municipal elections in 1862.

Working women and the oldest profession

On the whole, women's employment opportunities, an important key to greater equality, remained poor throughout the 19th century. In the countryside, unmarried women could make a little extra money by spinning at home (hence the term 'spinster') but many of those who married had to work in the fields all day as well as keeping house, just to keep the family above the poverty line. The work and the strain of child-bearing sent many to a premature grave.

In the towns, too, things were bad. Only the lucky few could find factory jobs, working for a pittance as sweated labour. Trapped between few jobs and poor wages, many women turned to prostitution.

This was a dangerous occupation, with a great risk of contracting venereal disease. On the other hand, Bernard Shaw's play of the 1890s, *Mrs Warren's Profession,* was undoubtedly correct in asserting that working class girls were better off working as prostitutes than in the white-lead factories where many died from phosphorous poisoning.

Absurd views about sex prevailed. For example, in 1870 American medical science suggested that men should not make love to their wives more than once a month. Indulgence was thought to be both sinful and harmful. Besides, contraceptives were primitive (and thought to be immoral), the birth rate was often more than the mother's health could stand and more than the father's wage could support. As a result, the demand for prostitutes was high.

It has been estimated that one in ten Americans was afflicted with venereal disease at the turn of the century. The situation was not much better in Britain. The government sought to reduce the problem by introducing the Contagious Diseases Act, which allowed for the compulsory medical inspection of women suspected of being prostitutes.

Women displayed remarkable solidarity in opposing this Act. Thousands joined Josephine Butler's campaign which secured its repeal after a 15-year struggle. This victory showed women that they could win concessions from a male-dominated world. But though the campaign succeeded, the double standard remained: the prostitute was a social outcast, her clients were not.

This exemplifies the entrenched inequality of the sexes against which the suffragettes had to fight. Examples of male attitudes make amusing reading today. One eminent doctor suggested in *The London Times* that half the female population went mad as a result of the menopause, and he regarded the Suffragette Movement as proof of it: 'There are no good women, but only women who have lived under the influence of good men.' An early criminologist, Lombroso, went further and stated, 'even the normal woman is a half-criminaloid being'.

However, the women's cause was not helped by some of the equally extreme statements of its leaders. One suffragette wrote '. . . sterilization is a higher form of human achievement than repro-duction.' Such expressions left the movement open

William Holman Hunt 'The Awakening Conscience': The Tate Gallery, London

The Mansell Collection

to accusations of lesbianism and unnaturalness.

In America, some preoccupations of the women's movement worked against it. It was staunchly in favour of the temperance movement and advocated the prohibition of alcohol. Many felt that 'votes for women' was synonymous with prohibition for men.

Many men were satisfied with the prevailing state of affairs. Enfranchizing women did not promise any improvement. Nevertheless, important inroads were being made on their complacency. An attack on the existing structure of marriage was beginning. Ibsen's play, *The Doll's House,* poured scorn on the hypocrisy of an outwardly happy marriage where the husband was head of the household, and the woman's place was in the home. In *Dance of Death* (1901), August Strindberg portrayed the misery of an unhappy marriage. E. M. Forster described, in *The Longest Journey* (1907), a man whose soul is destroyed by marriage.

Many marriages were unhappy, of course, and extremely difficult to dissolve. In England, for example, adultery by the husband was only grounds for divorce when accompanied by cruelty. The problem was worst for the middle classes. The upper classes could manage financially, if not socially, with the cost of ending a marriage; many of the urban

The introduction of typewriters to offices and the employment of thousands of young, literate women to operate them, originally helped many to find social and financial independence, as well as entry into the previously closed world of commerce.

working classes did not bother with a formal wedding ceremony, so there was no need for a formal divorce if the relationship soured. The movement for easier divorce, advocated as much by men as by women, achieved early success in America and France.

H. G. Wells' *Ann Veronica* told of the story of a young woman's struggle for independence, equality with men, and sexual freedom. The old attitudes about sex had at last come into question. The Victorian ethos found it desirable that a respectable woman knew nothing about sex; she was certainly not supposed to enjoy it. But the turn of the century brought new ideas. Havelock Ellis, the outspoken psychologist, wrote that women had erotic feelings of their own. Freud's psychological work gradually aroused public interest. Thus, easier divorce, a growing awareness of birth control and freedom from repressive sexual guilt, all added up to women's greater independence.

Trailblazers

The success of individual Victorian women in making a name for themselves also paved the way for later success. Florence Nightingale was one such woman. By organizing hospitals in the Crimea during the war of 1854–56, and later by becoming an adviser to the government on nursing, she made a significant step forward for women.

Amantine Dupin under her pen-name George Sand gained fame for her novels. Sarah Bernhardt

Mrs Emmeline Pankhurst (below), founder of the Women's Social and Political Union, fought militantly for women's right to vote. She undoubtedly captured attention though her violent enterprises jeopardized wider public support.

attracted great fame as an actress, and Elizabeth Garratt Anderson fought a long but successful battle to be admitted by Edinburgh University to study medicine. She qualified in 1865.

Such notable individuals showed what was possible, but the grass roots of the suffragette movement grew as a result of growing job opportunities for middle-class women. The 1871 Education Act created many jobs for women, as teachers.

High standards of respectablity were demanded of women teachers. The expectation was for them to be unmarried and to behave as though they had taken vows of poverty, chastity and obedience. Some teacher training colleges in the 1880s refused to install baths on the grounds that it would be unwise to give the teachers a standard of living they would never again be able to afford. Nevertheless, the large number of women employed in teaching played an important part, later on, in the fight to gain the vote.

The fundamental change came, however, with the expansion of office work. The advent of the

H. H. Asquith (below), took the post of Prime Minister in 1908, with a strong personal antipathy to the Women's Movement. He held power for eight years, and though he gradually accepted women's suffrage as inevitable, he staved it off for a decade.

typewriter drew thousands of women into offices. The introduction of the telephone also created a demand for switchboard operators. Office work in the 20th century replaced domestic service as the main employer of women. More jobs, and the new nature of those jobs, meant more independence.

In the home, the advent of tinned food, electric light, floor sweepers and soap flakes all lessened the drudgery of housework. And so at last, social and economic changes over a long period of time had created an environment in which the fight for the vote stood a reasonable chance of success.

Catching the public eye

The birthplace of the movement was the radical centre of Britain – Manchester. In 1903, a 45-year-old widow named Emmeline Pankhurst formed the Women's Social and Political Union (WSPU). 'Social' did not signify a programme of tea-parties, but referred to Pankhurst's socialism: the WSPU was allied to the Independent Labour Party.

The WSPU realised that polite lobbying of MPs was useless. Public opinion had first to be aroused. In October 1905, Emmeline Pankhurst, her eldest daughter Christabel and Annie Kenny were charged with attempting to cause a disturbance at a political meeting. They chose to be imprisoned rather than pay a small fine. For the first time, the public and press took notice.

At the general election of January 1906 the Liberal Party won a landslide victory. Believing the Liberals would be more sympathetic to the cause of the WSPU, the Pankhursts moved to London. They organized a procession from the statue of Queen Boudicca on Westminster Bridge to 10 Downing Street for the benefit of Prime Minister Sir Henry

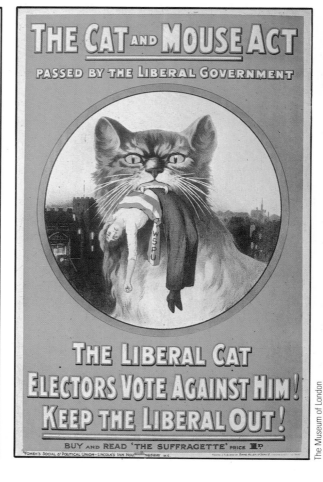

The first instances of suffragette violence sparked off no more than the predictable laughter, as a postcard of 1908 shows (top left). When the women began to reap much worse violence in return at the hands of the authorities, they attracted far more sympathy for their cause. The government's clumsy methods – force feeding, and the cat-and-mouse release and re-arrest act – proved self-defeating. Suffragette campaigners were not slow to exploit their suffering, in pamphlets and electioneering posters (left).

The National Gallery, London

In 1914, a suffragette protester slashed a canvas in the National Gallery. She chose Velazquez' Rokeby Venus (left), a priceless art treasure but one which epitomizes the age-old masculine view of women – simply objects of desire.

Campbell-Bannerman. Campbell-Bannerman was sympathetic, but the Cabinet was divided on the issue. The main opposition centred on Chancellor Herbert Asquith.

Then came heartening news from overseas. In 1902 Australia gave women the vote. In 1907 Norway followed suit. Ellen Kay, a Swedish social reformer received a favourable response to her calls for state maternity benefits – benefits explicitly extended to unmarried mothers. Such successes did a lot to sway British public opinion. The strength of the suffragette movement came not with more and more activists and demonstrations, but in the groundswell of supporters.

Setbacks and schisms

The movement suffered a serious setback in 1908. Campbell-Bannerman resigned on grounds of ill-health and died almost immediately. Asquith took his place. However, he was well aware that the WSPU would pose a threat to the prestige and electoral position of his Government if the question was ignored. The fact remained that women could not be given the vote without affecting the political situation. Clearly extended suffrage might have to include all the voteless men as well.

The Conservative Party opposed the idea since so many poor people would be enfranchized. The Liberals also feared it would encourage the growth of the Labour Party. On the other hand, they were opposed to the Conservative idea of extending the vote only to a few property-owning women.

The WSPU itself, despite its professed socialism, was quite prepared to gain votes on the lines suggested by the Conservatives, feeling that votes for all women would follow, once the principles had been established. Policy and tactics within the WSPU were dominated by the Pankhurst family, though the political issue split even them. A younger daughter, Sylvia, remained convinced that the WSPU should remain a socialist, not just a feminist, movement.

In the summer of 1908, the WSPU held a series of impressive demonstrations. Emmeline and Christabel Pankhurst were arrested along with another leader, Mrs Drummond, in Trafalgar Square, and again chose to be imprisoned rather than bound over. In Bristol, one suffragette tried to attack Home Secretary Winston Churchill with a dog-whip, another hid inside the organ at the Albert Hall hoping to leap out during Asquith's speech. Another locked herself into Lloyd George's car and gave the Chancellor a long lecture before he was able to escape.

Prisoners and martyrs

Suffragettes became more of an embarrassment to the authorities when imprisoned campaigners started hunger strikes. Initially, the government released them rather than offend public opinion by letting women starve. But this course seemed too weak. Force-feeding the women prisoners was suggested as the only solution. Churchill was cautious. He wanted to retain the support of Irish MPs, some of whom had experienced such handling as political prisoners of the 1880s. No matter how well supervized, force-feeding was a terrible business: a tube forced up the nostrils by one doctor and food poured down it by another. At least one prisoner was driven insane by the process.

The government line softened. Asquith had enough problems in facing two elections in 1910. During the run up to the December election, he promised to introduce a bill to extend male franchise, with an amendment to include women as well. In 1911, the WSPU called off its campaign of violence and looked forward to the Liberals fulfilling their promise. But Asquith seemed to be wavering again. And radicals in the WSPU bridled at the thought of votes for women passing into law as an afterthought. Emmeline Pankhurst returned from a tour of America and incited a large meeting of women in Parliament Square to go out and smash windows in protest. A week later, the idea was put into effect. In the early hours of 1 March 1912 around 200 women smashed most of the shop windows in London's Piccadilly, Regent Street and Oxford Street. Emmeline Pankhurst herself went to Downing Street to break Asquith's. Most of the women were arrested. Christabel Pankhurst, her mother in prison, fled to Paris.

In April 1912, the Commons rejected the Bill to extend franchise. The window smashing episode had lost vital support. More to the point, however, the Irish MPs had changed their mind and opposed the Bill, since they felt it would cost so much parliamentary time as to jeopardize Home Rule for Ireland.

The main body of support for the women's cause inside Parliament came from the Labour Party. One Labour member, George Lansbury even resigned his seat and stood for re-election as a WSPU candidate. Politically, he had cut his own throat: he failed.

After Lansbury's failure, many in the WSPU began to feel that alliance with the Conservative party might at least win them a limited extension of the vote to women property-owners. This feeling grew when Asquith withdrew a second bill to enfranchize all men (with women included in an amendment) on a technicality. In her prison cell, Emmeline Pankhurst felt betrayed.

In early 1913 the suffragettes turned to violence more stridently. They burnt a few country railway stations; put a bomb into a house being built for Lloyd George; mutilated the greens of golf clubs with acid; poured acid into post boxes; and slashed the Rokeby Venus in the National Gallery. Fortunately, no-one was killed as a result of their actions, or the movement could have been irrevocably destroyed.

Such militancy led to further arrests and, in turn, more hunger strikes. The Government dealt with the

This picture – originally captioned 'The Amazons-of-the-Vote are expelled from the Palace of Westminster' (right) – was published in the Italian press in 1906. Europe watched, with vested interest, the evolution of women's suffrage in Britain.

Protest turned to tragedy at the 1913 Derby when suffragette Emily Davidson threw herself in front of the galloping field and was trampled to death by the King's horse, Anmer (right). She was looked upon by her fellow suffragettes as a heroine and a martyr.

The heroic efforts of women who took over the jobs of men during World War I, particularly in the munitions factories (right), proved once and for all their equality and natural right to the vote. During the war years virtually all suffragette protest stopped, which perhaps helped smooth the path to suffrage when it finally came in 1918.

embarrassment by releasing hunger strikers and rearresting them when they had recovered their strength: the law was nicknamed the 'Cat and Mouse Act'. Emmeline Pankhurst was constantly rearrested after release: she had been reduced by her efforts to such a state of weakness that she had to be released after only a day or two's hunger strike. She also suffered from a gastric complaint which worsened her health. The authorities were terrified in case she died in custody. Her death would fuel the fury of the women's movement without robbing it of a leader: it could be run from the safety of Paris by Christabel.

However, the suffragettes got their martyr in the summer of 1913. Emily Davidson – one of the first suffragettes to be arrested, for trying to set fire to a post box – had almost died for the cause while on hunger strike in Manchester. She had barricaded herself into her cell and been half drowned by warders who directed hose jets through the bars of her cell. On 4 June, Emily took a train to Epsom for the Derby – the most popular horse race in the sporting calendar. At Tattenham Corner she slipped under the railings and threw herself in front of a group of racing horses. She felled – almost certainly by chance – King George V's horse, Anmer, and was trampled to death.

Perhaps she did not expect to die: among her possessions the police found half a ticket, for the return train journey. Emmeline Pankhurst was rearrested when she attempted to attend the funeral, but despite her absence it was a great suffragette demonstration. The bands played solemn music by Chopin and Handel as the funeral cortege made its way from Victoria to Kings Cross railway station. The coffin, draped in the purple, green and white colours of the suffragettes, was put aboard the train, for burial at the Davidson's home in Northumberland. At a service at St George's, Hanover Square, the suffragettes sang the hymn *Fight the Good Fight*.

Briefly the women's movement was united by Emily's sacrifice. But while Emmeline and Christabel Pankhurst moved progressively to the political right, Sylvia Pankhurst was preaching socialism in the East End of London. Mother and elder sister felt that such idealism detracted from the movement and deterred many of the more middle class suffragettes who contributed to the movement's funds. Sylvia was therefore expelled from the WSPU by her mother. But when, in June 1914, Asquith at last agreed to receive a suffragette delegation, the invitation was extended to Sylvia Pankhurst's East London Federation for Women's Suffrage, not the WSPU. Asquith, who was gradually accepting the inevitability of women's suffrage, had decided to

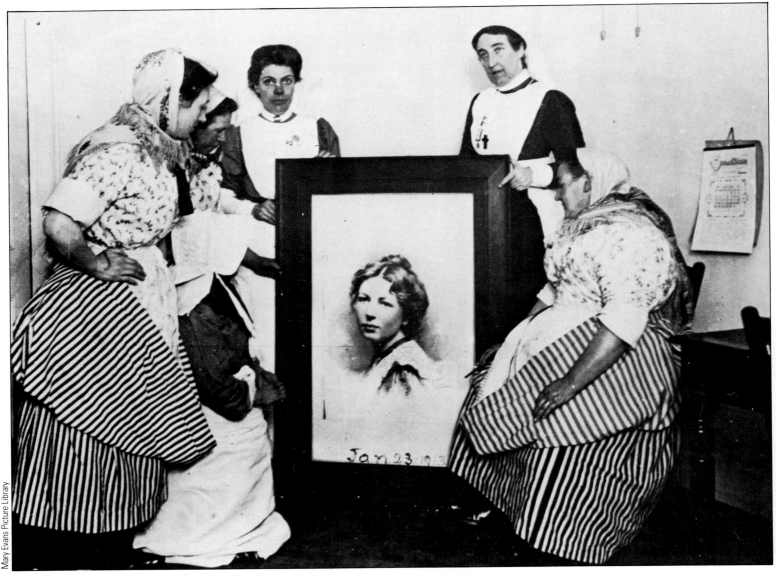

Members of the Women's Social and Political Union (WSPU) gather round a portrait of Christabel Pankhurst, daughter of Emmeline and heiress apparent to the WSPU leadership.

court popularity with working class women, in the hope they would vote Liberal, not Labour. The Prime Minister did not commit himself: he simply succeeded in giving the impression that the Government would shortly introduce a Bill for Universal Suffrage.

Women at war

Then, world events overtook both women and Government. Almost out of the blue, Britain was at war with Germany. World War I had begun.

The women's movement plunged into the war effort. The WSPU leadership were prominent in patriotic activity and ready to shelve the vote. No doubt they felt, like everyone else, that the war would be a short interlude, 'over by Christmas'.

In the event, the war delayed votes for women for four long years. But at the end of it, in 1918, six million women were enfranchised. It has been suggested that women received the vote because of their contribution to the war effort. But their war efforts only added the finishing touches. Women were admired for working in the munitions industries, running the risk of being blown to pieces. But the war was not the first time women had contributed to industry and they had worked in far worse conditions before the war.

When Parliament again considered the vote for women in 1918, so many men had been killed in the trenches that universal suffrage would have meant women voters outnumbering men. It was therefore suggested that all men should have the vote at 21, but women should not receive it until they were 30. Many of the leaders of the movement stood as candidates in the 1918 election, but only one woman MP was returned to Parliament: Countess Makievicz was elected as Sinn Fein member for South Dublin by electors with causes other than feminism on their minds. Women did not vote to see women elected: they tended to fall in line with their husbands: people went on voting according to their class.

The 30-year age limit remained in force till 1928 when complete equality was achieved. Emmeline Pankhurst died on 4 June 1928, just as Royal Assent was given to the Act.

No doubt the suffragettes would have been disappointed to see the poor representation of women in government, commerce and industry today. But their fight for votes did demonstrate to women that this and similar goals could be achieved in a male dominated society. Gradually, greater (though not complete) equality with men has been achieved. Undoubtedly these advances owe much to the efforts of the suffragettes and their brave forerunners.

THE GREAT COMPOSERS

Joaquín Rodrigo

b. 1901

Beethoven once described the guitar as a 'miniature orchestra'; perhaps no composer has elevated the guitar's status as a serious concert instrument more than Spain's Joaquín Rodrigo. His rich works and deep understanding of the instrument helped to establish a successful relationship between guitar and orchestra. Rodrigo composed many types of work, but it is his brilliant guitar concertos which capture the very essence of his Spanish homeland. His passionate and haunting Concierto de Aranjuez and the striking Fantasia para un Gentilhombre, both analysed in the Listener's Guide, *were great successes and led to his world-wide acclaim. Ironically, Rodrigo composed the Concierto de Aranjuez in exile in Paris, for the Spain he had pictured so vividly had been torn by a bitter civil war. In* The Background *describes the three brutal years of struggle between the forces of Socialism and Fascism.*

Joaquín Rodrigo was blind from an early age, but he overcame the physical and practical difficulties to become one of Spain's finest composers. He studied harmony and composition in Valencia and premiered his first orchestral work there before entering the l'Ecole Normale de Musique in Paris in 1927. He earned much respect for his nostalgic, tender works, and was awarded a scholarship to continue to study in Paris, thus escaping the brutality of Spain's Civil War. His Concierto de Aranjuez was premiered in 1940, winning him great acclaim. He and his wife, the pianist Victoria Kamhi, returned to Madrid, where he continued to compose and also became involved in music education and Spanish radio. In 1958, he travelled to America to attend the first world performance of the Fantasia para un Gentilhombre. The recipient of numerous international awards and tributes, Rodrigo continues to live and write in Madrid.

COMPOSER'S LIFE

'Un gentilhombre'

Overcoming the physical and practical difficulties of blindness, the Spanish composer Joaquin Rodrigo has successfully pursued a musical career and produced, along the way, the world-famous guitar concertos.

Colourful and picturesque, the music of Spanish composer Joaquín Rodrigo belies the tragic fact that he has been almost blind from early childhood.

The youngest of Juana and Vincente Rodrigo's ten children, Joaquín was born in the Valencian town of Sagunto (eastern Spain) on 22 November 1901. Quite appropriately, for one destined to be so musically gifted, he shares his birthday with St Cecilia – the patron saint of music.

In 1905, when Rodrigo was just three years old, Sagunto was hit by a diphtheria epidemic – then a deadly disease. Many of the town's children died and though Rodrigo caught and survived the illness, it left him with badly damaged eyesight. After many operations, including an iris graft, he was able to differentiate light and bright colours, and later when he was an adult, he had another operation in which a corneal graft was undertaken. Sadly, although his opthalmologist had felt confident he would see again, only weeks after the operation it became clear that because of glaucoma he would never regain his sight.

Rodrigo has never considered himself in any way handicapped by his blindness, and through his fortitude along with the devotion of one of his father's employees, Rafael Ibanēz, and then later, of his wife, Victoria Kamhi, the world has been able to share in his musical creativity.

Childhood memories

Of his childhood in Sagunto, Rodrigo remembers particularly the sounds around him – the sounds of the cicadas buzzing in the night and the sounds of the church organ at Sagunto. One of his most vivid memories is of the sheep his father gave him to play with. He remembers playing with it as if it were a donkey, pulling it around la Glorieta, the main square of Sagunto.

In 1906 the family moved from Sagunto to Valencia, the capital of the province. Soon after, when he was seven, his parents sent him to a school for blind children where he studied all the usual subjects plus piano and music which he studied in braille. At school his musical talent was quickly recognized and nurtured by his music teachers.

When he was a youngster, Rodrigo was looked after by one of his father's employees, Rafael Ibanēz. Although not a particularly cultured man he learned everything that was necessary to help Rodrigo, and for many years was his valet, secretary and music copyist. Of him Rodrigo said, 'He lent me his eyes'.

Rodrigo loved music from as far back as he can remember although, apart from one of his sisters who played piano, no one else in the family was at all musical. His feelings were confirmed when he heard a performance on the clavichord by the Polish artist Wanda Landowska, which moved him deeply. And the first time he heard *Rigoletto* he knew that music was to be his metier. By the time he was 16 the idea of making a living from life as a musician or composer was firmly set in his mind. Thus, in 1917, Rodrigo began harmony and composition studies with Francisco Antich in Valencia, despite the opposition of his father – a merchant and landowner. Rodrigo's determination to pursue music must have been strong indeed, for he remembers his father as a formidable person.

My father was very tough and we were all frightened of him. I used to be very obedient. He did not want me to study much and especially not

Joaquín Rodrigo (aged six months), left, was the tenth child of Juana and Vincente Rodrigo. He was born in 1901 in Sagunto (above), a town in the Spanish province of Valencia. His childhood was marred by an epidemic of diphtheria which killed many children in the town. Rodrigo was three when he contracted the disease and it left his eyesight severely damaged. Despite several operations in his childhood and later when he was an adult, he became completely blind.

music. Thank God, for once, I did not listen to him. We would have been without a penny all our lives!

At this time, too, he came into contact with Eduardo Chavarri and Enrique Gomá, both composers and music critics, who became friends and advisers to him. While studying with Antich, Rodrigo wrote several orchestral compositions. In 1924 his first major work *Juglares* (Minstrels) was given a public performance by the Valencia Symphony Orchestra. His parents did not attend and Rodrigo, probably too strong in character to ask the reason why, has never known for sure whether they were afraid he would not succeed, or whether they were genuinely set against his choice of career. However, regardless of this lack of parental support Rodrigo went on to win further acclaim, particularly with the first public performance of the piano and orchestral work, *Cinco piezas infantiles* in 1925.

The Paris years

Despite Rodrigo's early success, it was clear to his tutors and mentors that he still needed to broaden his horizons. So, following in the footsteps of many other Spanish composers including Albeniz, Granados and Manuel de Falla, he went to study in Paris. In 1927, aged 26, he enrolled in Paul Dukas's composition class at l'Ecole Normale de Musique. Dukas, a contemporary of Debussy and mainly remembered as the composer of the tone poem *The Sorcerer's Apprentice,* was highly regarded as a teacher. Rodrigo quickly became a favourite pupil and studied with him for five years. Rodrigo came to the sophisticated city as a composer who reflected his

Rodrigo's musical talent was fostered by his teachers and in 1925, notwithstanding the acclaim received by his early compositions, they felt that he should study abroad. So he enrolled at L'Ecole Normale *in Paris, where he studied with Paul Dukas (right, front row third from left). In moving to Paris, Rodrigo followed in the footsteps of many other Spanish composers including Granados (below) and Manuel de Falla (below right). The latter was to be a major influence on Rodrigo's life and music.*

Collection Joaquín Rodrigo/Photo Christopher Barker

J de la Torre 'Portrait of Enrique Granados'/Edistudio

Vazquez Diaz 'Manuel de Falla'/Arxiu Mas

background – a background of warm native passions and rural Mediterranean life – and this soon shone through in his work. In the light of this, Dukas, a sceptical, witty and cultivated man, proved to be an ideal teacher, for while he spurred Rodrigo on, he curbed his natural youthful tendency 'to run wild as a composer'. And as a Spanish commentator later remarked, Rodrigo learned from Dukas 'that familiar blend of irony and tenderness.' In practical terms he helped Rodrigo to get his music performed. Indeed, Rodrigo premièred several works at recitals in the private homes of many wealthy patrons who were introduced to him by Dukas. In this way he was able to ease his often difficult financial circumstances.

As well as studying, Rodrigo was naturally plunged into the cultural whirlpool of life in Paris. He met most of the major contemporary figures in music – among them Albert Roussel, the pianist Alfred Cortot, Vincent d'Indy, Jacques Ibert, Arthur Honegger,

Darius Milhaud, Maurice Ravel and Stravinsky.

Most of Rodrigo's close friends at this time were Spanish. As well as his secretary Rafael Ibanéz, who was also in Paris, he was particularly friendly with the guitarist Emilio Pujol, the pianist Ricardo Vinés and his fellow student Jesus Arambarri. It was through his teacher Dukas that Rodrigo met the renowned Spanish composer, Manuel de Falla. The friendship and counsel of Falla, then in his fifties, had a decisive influence on Rodrigo's life and future development. Falla's encouragement is reflected in many works of the late 1920s and early 30s, when Rodrigo's special musical voice first began to be heard.

In 1928 Rodrigo met a beautiful Ottoman-Turkish pianist, Victoria Kamhi who in 1933 became his wife. Their marriage had been foretold to her by a gypsy in Bucharest. The gist of this was that she would marry a famous man with a name beginning with 'Jo'. She gave up thinking about the prediction but one day

While a student in Paris, Rodrigo met the beautiful pianist Victoria Kamhi (above left). She had been told by a gypsy that she would marry a famous man whose name began with the letters 'Jo'. The prophecy came true in 1933 when she and Joaquin Rodrigo (above) were married in Valencia. Victoria Kamhi's devotion to her husband and diligence in the day-to-day running of their lives together is enduring. Rodrigo asserts in heart-warming tones that 'she has shared his life, his hunger, his work and his glory'.

In 1938 Rodrigo returned to study in Paris, this time on a scholarship arranged by Manuel de Falla. Rodrigo felt confident enough about his maturing style to begin work on a major composition, the **Concierto de Aranjuez** *(Rodrigo holding original title page, left). The inspiration for the work was the atmosphere of 18th-century Spanish life in general and in particular the gardens and palace of Aranjuez (below).*

Gregorio Prieto/Photo Christopher Barker

Arxiu Mas

came across a piece of music by Rodrigo, *Prelude au Coq Matinal.* Although difficult to play she mastered it. Some time later, a friend of hers – Alexander Demetriad – asked her to translate a letter into German on behalf of a friend, and the friend turned out to be Rodrigo. Later, Demetriad arranged a meeting between them; Victoria played his prelude she had learnt earlier and, fulfilling the fortune-teller's story, they fell in love.

At first there were difficulties – they came from different national backgrounds and her parents objected to the match, but they prevailed over all the difficulties and from then on Victoria Kamhi became his closest collaborator. Her diligence both in the day-to-day organization of their lives and in the preparation of his music is obvious and heart-warming. Today Rodrigo states with affection and conviction that she has shared his life, his hunger, his work, his glory.

Return to Spain

Their marriage, celebrated in Valencia in 1933, heralded a short return to Spain. Rodrigo's hard work in France was beginning to be rewarded as his reputation spread. He was nominated for a professor's chair at the College for the Blind in Madrid (but never took up the appointment) and his new symphonic poem *Per la flor del Lliri blau* had its première in Valencia. Most important of all, however, through the benign machinations of Falla, he was awarded the *Conde de Cartagena* scholarship which enabled him to return to Paris for a further two years of study. Rodrigo asserts that it is thanks to Falla and the scholarship that he was away from Spain during the horrific Civil War – a conflict he believes he may not have survived.

In exile

On his return to Paris, Rodrigo studied the history of music with Maurice-Emmanuel at the Conservatoire and with Andre Pirro at the Sorbonne – his former teacher Dukas was too ill to take him on as a pupil again (Dukas died in 1935). That year Rodrigo wrote a piano sonata, *Sonada de Adios,* in memory of and in tribute to Paul Dukas.

With the outbreak of civil war in Spain, Rodrigo's state scholarship was withdrawn. Victoria's parents helped them and she worked as a music copyist. He stayed in Paris for a while, then Freiburg and Salzburg. These were far from ideal circumstances for creativity, but his growing maturity and the awareness that his style was becoming more and more fully formed gave him confidence to begin a major work. In 1938, on his return to Paris, he began work on the *Concierto de Aranjuez.* The work was ready for its first performance late in 1940, by which time the Civil War was over and the Rodrigos had once more taken up residence in Madrid.

Honours and acclaim

For the next ten years Rodrigo's life was comparatively settled. He was happy working and living in Madrid, and in 1941 his only daughter, Cecilia, was born. During this time he was hard at work producing a steady stream of compositions including, in 1942, the *Concierto Heroico* and in 1943, the *Concierto de Estio.*

His career expanded into other areas, as well, all related to his musical creativity. In 1944 he was appointed to the post of Artistic Director of Spain's national radio and four years later was appointed to the newly created Manuel de Falla Chair of Music at the University of Madrid. In 1949 he travelled to Argentina for a Rodrigo Festival at the Teatro Colon in Buenos Aires. Further honours followed in the 1950s: he was appointed a member of the Royal Academy of Fine Arts of San Fernando and in 1954 was elected Vice-President of the Spanish section of the Société International de Musique Contemporaine. Also in 1954 he renewed his acquaintance with the guitarist, Segovia, whom he had met in 1929 in Paris during his student days. At that time Rodrigo and Segovia discussed the possibility of the latter playing one of Rodrigo's compositions. Circumstances – the Spanish Civil War and World War II – probably prevented Segovia from playing the *Concierto de Aranjuez* when it was first written. However, Rodrigo dedicated the *Fantasia para un Gentil-hombre* to him – feeling it was a fitting compliment to the man he regarded as the 'Gentleman of the Guitar of our days'.

Between 1955 and 1958 he produced three more large-scale works: the music for the ballet *Pavana Real* to a scenario by his wife; the *Concierto serenata* for harp and orchestra; and the orchestral work, *Musica para un jardin*.

Joaquin Rodrigo (above), using a braille typewriter, at work on the composition of Concierto Heroico *for piano and orchestra which was successfully premièred in 1942.*

Rodrigo with the British cellist, Julian Lloyd-Webber (above left), for whom he composed a cello concerto.

Camera Press

International reputation
Rodrigo's international reputation continued to grow and in 1958 he travelled to America where Segovia gave the first world performance of the *Fantasia para un Gentilhombre*.

His last religious work *Himnos nupciales* (Wedding Hymn) had a very personal première in April 1963 at the wedding of his daughter Cecilia to the violinist Agostin Leon Ara. Later in the year Rodrigo's travels took him to Puerto Rico where he delivered a course in music history at the University. By 1973 Rodrigo's reputation had reached Japan where his music was celebrated with a series of Rodrigo Festivals in various Japanese cities. Elsewhere, he has been showered with further tributes: streets were named after him; his home town endowed the Rodrigo prize for choral composition; he was awarded the Cross of the *Légion d'Honneur*; the French government made him an Officier des Arts et des Lettres; and he also

received an honorary doctorate from the University of Salamanca.

Rodrigo, an excellent pianist and violinist, is known all over the world mainly for the wonderful music he has written for the guitar, an instrument on which in his own words he cannot play 'four notes in a row'. It is often said that once a blind musician has overcome and learned to live with his handicap, as Rodrigo's resilient and remarkable personality has certainly enabled him to do, his awareness of the world of sound and hearing becomes finely tuned and intensely responsive. Rodrigo's ability to know how to reproduce what he hears in his mind on paper has revolutionized guitar technique. His method of working takes a long time and is, therefore, costly but as far as he knows he is the only composer who writes all his scores, not only for single instruments but also for the whole orchestration, in braille. After he has completed the whole work in braille he dictates it to a copyist – at one time

Collection Joaquin Rodrigo

In 1954 Rodrigo dedicated the Fantasia para un Gentilhombre *(title page left), to the renowned Spanish guitarist Segovia. The work was inspired by themes of a 17th century guitarist Gaspar Sanz, and in the work Rodrigo pays homage to both Sanz and Segovia.*

Collection Joaquin Rodrigo

Joaquin Rodrigo and his wife Victoria (below) continue to live in an apartment in Madrid. As ever, music, whether it is in the concert hall or on record or in the shape of his own compositions, is still the mainspring of his life.

Photo Christopher Barker

his old friend Rafael Ibanẽz. Rodrigo was once greatly offended by a questioner who asked Victoria if Rodrigo 'whistled the *Concierto de Aranjuez* and then someone else did the orchestration?'

As well as the many orchestral and instrumental compositions he has written during his life, Rodrigo has produced over 60 songs. He feels that in his song or *lied* writing, the composer he comes closest to is the Viennese Romantic composer, Franz Schubert. Rodrigo, however, does not see himself as a Romantic, more as a traditionalist composer. Today's composers, Rodrigo feels, lack the ability to create as many melodies in their compositions as he and his predecessors did. This is one of the reasons, he believes, for the great popularity of one of his own melodically beautiful compositions, *Concierto de Aranjuez,* which is reputed to be one of the best selling records in the world.

At home, in Madrid

Rodrigo lives, as he has done for many years, in a modern apartment in the centre of Madrid. He spends much of his time reading braille books or listening to books on cassettes, as well as to his wife reading to him. Both he and his wife enjoy concerts and theatre-going, and find pleasure in taking long walks together. Time spent with their friends and family, which includes their two grand-daughters, Cecilia and Patricia, is precious to them.

Listening to and composing music, as ever, is still the driving force of his life. Among the instrumental soloists for whom he has written music are the guitarists John Williams and Julian Bream, the cellist Julian Lloyd-Webber and the flautist James Galway. Rodrigo has most recently worked on a fantasia called *Old Romances without Words.*

Guitar concertos

Rodrigo's guitar concertos, with their folk-music motifs arranged within a classical framework, have helped to elevate the guitar's status to that of a serious concert instrument.

Beethoven is said to have described the guitar as a 'miniature orchestra', a tribute to its ability to produce a wide range of tone-colours. But in spite of its great expressive capabilities, before Rodrigo none of the few guitar concertos that had been attempted had really worked. When a guitar is pitched against even a small orchestra as a solo instrument, it inevitably faces the problem of not being heard. Consequently, the guitar had almost always been used an instrument for small-scale pieces. Although modern amplification techniques have now helped change this situation, it was, first and foremost, Rodrigo's unique skill in composing for the instrument that established a truly successful relationship between guitar and orchestra.

Concierto de Aranjuez
In 1939 Rodrigo wrote what was to become one of the most famous concertos of the century – the *Concierto de Aranjuez*. The idea of writing a concerto for guitar came to him at the suggestion of his friend, Spanish guitar virtuoso, Regino Sainz de la Maza (1897–1982). Rodrigo's *Concierto de Aranjuez* was first performed in Barcelona (December 1940) with Sainz de la Maza as the soloist. What had first seemed impossible, because of the problems of setting a guitar against an orchestra, turned out to be a huge success. Public and critical acclaim was immediate and it led to the world-wide fame of both the work and its composer.

Two reasons lie behind the titling of the work: 'Aranjuez' was the summer palace of the 18th-century Bourbon Kings of Spain, built some 45 miles south of Madrid. The palace represented to Rodrigo his favourite period in history and the music is intended to evoke an epoch in the life of Aranjuez, that of the last two pre-Napoleonic Kings – 'Subtly characterized by *majas* (young women) and bull-fighters, and by Spanish-American tunes' as Rodrigo puts it. Rodrigo was also attached to Aranjuez for nostalgic reasons – during their courtship, he and Victoria had spent much time walking together in the palace's beautiful gardens – and of the music's interpretation says:

The Aranjuez Concerto is meant to sound like the hidden breeze that stirs in the treetops and parks, and it should only be as strong as a butterfly and as dainty as a veronica.

The Concerto's tremendous popularity when it first appeared was perhaps due in part to its novelty, but its lasting strength lies in its success in painting a stunning sound-picture of Spain and its national heritage. For the guitar is steeped in Spain's folk tradition and through the instrument Rodrigo manages to capture the colour, mood, melody and parodox of Mediterranean life, where gaiety can be suddenly transformed into great sadness.

The work has the air of music 'written out of its time' with its distilled essence of warmly romanticized folk-musical forms and idioms linked together through a classical style of composition.

Programme notes
The *Concierto de Aranjuez* is scored for strings, woodwind and brass (trumpets/horns), providing a rich palette of tone-colours.

First movement – Allegro con spirito
Within the classical framework of sonata form, the movement evokes a folk-musical dance, the *fandango,* a sprightly courtship dance from the heart of Spain. As the work opens, the attention is focused immediately on the soloist, the guitar beginning above a quiet note in the basses. The opening passage uses a rhythmic device that pervades the entire movement, six quavers being divided into either two threes (6/8, the basic time of the movement) or three twos (3/4 time, as in the second bar).

Example 1

This, the *hemiola,* in which the stress varies but not the bar length, giving a syncopated rhythm, is found in much Spanish folk music and in renaissance and baroque dances from all over Europe.

The guitar moves into a *staccato ostinato* figure (where the notes are persistently detached) with quiet comment from the woodwind, after which the strings take over the opening passage. Above the subdued chatter a bold subject enters (oboe/violins), soon varied by the guitar and extended in a perky dialogue with the woodwind. This in turn leads into an extended *Phrygian cadence* (chords of E minor and F sharp major), characteristic of flamenco music, and then to a new

Sorolla 'Romería Gallega' The hispanic Society of America. Arxiu Mas

*Andres Segovia
(above) was one of
the world's best
loved guitarists,
and was largely
responsible for the
present popularity
of the guitar. In the
years following
World War I,
feeling a great lack
in the guitar's
repertoire, he
travelled all over
the world as its
evangelist, pressing
composers who
were not guitarists
to write for it. One
such composer was
Joaquin Rodrigo
who later
dedicated his
Fantasia para un
Gentilhombre to
him.*

*It is the
quintessential
Spanishness of
Rodrigo's guitar
works, with their
strong colour,
sense of history
and tradition of
his native land
(left), that has
helped make them
so popular and
appealing.*

The second movement of the Concierto de Aranjuez, *Adagio, evokes the atmosphere of the annual Holy Week procession in Seville –* The Saeta *(left).*

theme announced by the guitar (a bassoon supplying the bass).

Example 2

Unusually, each theme has so far entered in the tonic key (D major), but the recently introduced material now passes through the more remote regions of F and D-flat major, arriving in A minor, whose dominant chord is crowned with a spinning figure and a rapid, descending run. The development begins, in the same key, with a return of the *fandango* rhythm in the strings. The treatment of the thematic material is very clear and it involves the guitar in much rapid passage-work and chord-strumming (*rasgueado*). A swirling, downward scale (woodwind/upper strings) leads to the recapitulation which, like the exposition, ends with guitar pyrotechnics in the dominant chord of D major. The coda is based largely on the earlier *staccato ostinato* figure first introduced by the guitar; and though it reaches a joyous *tutti* (where the orchestra takes over from the solo guitar) it ends quietly, the guitar referring briefly to the *fandango* rhythm.

Second movement – Adagio
The guitar, above a sustained bass in the lower strings, sets the scene by simple repetitions of the tonic chord of B minor; after one bar, the English horn sings the plaintive melody by which the Concerto is best known. This is the sound of the *Saeta,*

The colour and spirit of Spain's folk music, expressed through the syncopated rhythms of traditional flamenco songs and dances (left) – pervades **Concierto de Aranjuez.**

Understanding music: Spanish music

It is not surprising that the music of Spain is indissolubly linked with the guitar: its role is deeply interwoven in the history of Spanish music. And its pre-eminence as a typically Spanish instrument has arisen out of Spain's unusual and very rich folk tradition.

Up to the 13th century, Spain was subjected to many foreign influences, the most lasting of which – and the one which most distinguished Spanish culture from that of European neighbours – was the Moorish occupation, which endured for nearly five centuries. This left Spain with a legacy of exotic oriental modes, and rhythms and dances which survived as the folk tradition.

The Moslem invaders also introduced new musical instruments to Spain, including the Arabic 'ud, or lute, and castanets. From the lute the *vihuela* (a predecessor of the guitar) evolved and a condsiderable body of work was written for the instrument, particularly during the Renaissance. The guitar, though, for long the country-cousin of the more courtly vihuela, finally became the dominant instrument in the 17th century, capturing, as it did, the very essence of the Spanish folk idiom. Indeed its characteristic sound contributed to the nature of the keyboard works of Domenico Scarlatti, an Italian who spent most of his working life in Spain.

Later, composer/performers such as Fernando Sor (1778–1839) established new levels of technique and composing for the guitar which helped inspire a growing classical repertoire for the instrument. Antonio de Torres's re-appraisal of guitar design around 1870 established the shape and size of the modern classical guitar; while Francisco Tarrega (1852–1909) composed many works that widened the guitar's scope.

Spanish Nationalism
When most European countries were re-discovering and re-defining their national cultures during the Nationalist period of the late 19th century, Spain turned to its rich heritage of dance and, particularly, to the flamenco music of Andalusia with its stirring rhythms and red-blooded melodies that capture the proud, passionate spirit of Spanish folk music. Spain can boast of over 1,000 dance forms from its many regions – and most are accompanied by the guitar.

Felipe Pedrell (1841–1922) is considered the father of this renaissance. A composer and musicologist, he was tireless in his researches into the music of Spain's past and into the immensely convoluted world of folk music. Through his hands passed the first generation of Spanish nationalist composers, who led Spain into the mainstream of European music.

Isaac Albéniz (1860–1909), who stowed away at the age of twelve to South America and supported himself for a year by playing the piano in cafes and music halls in Argentina, Uruguay and Brazil, was a phenomenal pianist and studied for a while with Liszt. His work with Pedrell revealed to him the riches of Spanish music, which found its finest expression in his evocative suite of piano pieces, *Ibéria.*

Enrique Granados (1867–1916) studied with Pedrell at the same time as Albéniz and acknowledged with gratitude 'the nourishment of his precious counsel'. He is now best remembered for his piano suite, *Goyescas,* parts of which were reworked into an opera and performed to great acclaim in New York at the beginning of 1916. Following this success, a recital at the special request of President Wilson made him miss the boat returning directly to Spain. He returned via Liverpool, but the connecting boat to Dieppe was torpedoed by a German submarine. Granados, who had recently written to a friend: 'I have a whole world of ideas . . . I am only now starting my work', was drowned with his wife as he tried to rescue her.

The third composer of this 'school' was Manuel de Falla (1876–1946), and of the three, he is generally regarded as the most gifted. He studied with Pedrell from 1902 and described him as the 'cornerstone upon which modern Spanish music rests'. It is works like *Love the magician, The three-cornered hat* and *Night in the gardens of Spain* that most vividly convey the spirit of the nationalist movement and which have found lasting places in the repertories of orchestras throughout the world. Falla left Spain in 1939 as a result of the Civil War and spent the last seven years of his life in Argentina. There he worked as hard as his ill-health would allow on a huge oratorio, a miracle play called, *Atlantida* (Atlantis), which was unfinished when he died.

Spain, and especially its northern region of Catalonia, has also produced many great performers during the 20th century, such as the guitarist, Andrés Segovia and the cellist, Pablo Casals. Alicia de Larrocha is a virtually unmatched exponent of romantic Spanish piano music and singers such as Victoria de los Angeles, Monserrat Caballe and Teresa Berganza have been in demand throughout their careers by the top opera houses. More recently a young generation of tenors such as José Carreras and Francisco Araiza have captured audiences world wide.

the annual religious procession in which statues are carried through the streets of Seville, honouring the Virgin Mary. The nasal sound of the English horn evokes that of a *cantore* (flamenco singer). The melody, some notes of which are accented with mordents (inflecting on an adjacent note), is delivered in two sections. The guitar repeats each in turn, over a soft carpet of muted strings, adding its own florid, lyrical embellishments – as a *cantore* might. Short phrases taken from the melody then pass through the strings to the woodwind, leading to the key of E minor.

In this new key the guitar re-enters with a new phrase, on which the bassoon comments; the pattern continues through the remote keys of G minor and C minor, the oboe interposing reminders of the original tune. The orchestra intervenes, abruptly restoring the key of E minor; the guitar responds immediately with a solo on the opening melody. Another intervention (oboe/strings) turns the key toward A minor and stirs the guitar into passionate activity – long trills and rapid passage-work. As the passion subsides, it disperses into fast exchanges of fragmentary phrases (woodwind). The bassoon is left alone and a return to the key of G minor is implied. Surprisingly, the solo guitar begins a long cadenza in the key of G sharp minor, based on elements of the thematic materials and displaying a variety of arpeggios and other textures. Climactic *tremolando* chords (rapid iteration instead of holding) stir the full orchestra to return with the opening melody at full stretch, in the unexpected key of F sharp minor. The guitar resumes, gently leading the movement to a peaceful conclusion, ascending to its highest register above *pianissimo* strings. The closing chord of B major arrives like a shaft of evening sunshine.

Third movement – Allegro gentile

The final movement has the air of a courtly dance. Opening in B major the solo guitar immediately states the rondo theme in crisp two-part counterpoint. The irregular alternation of bars of 2/4 and 3/4 time creates variation of both stress and bar-length bringing a return to the syncopated style of the first movement. The orchestra promptly restates the theme but in D major, the 'home' key of the concerto.

The remainder of the movement may be divided into four episodes. In the first episode, the guitar delivers the subject in chords and continues to dominate, moving smoothly into another statement of the rondo, in continuous, *staccato* quivers, before modulating (or changing key) into

A collection of popular dances recorded by the Spanish baroque guitarist Gaspar Sanz provided the starting point for Rodrigo's Fantasia para un Gentilhombre. *The work opens with a* villano, *a rustic sung dance performed in the open air (right).*

C-sharp minor, in which the second episode commences. Strong, full guitar chords over *pizzicato* (plucked) lower strings are answered by the woodwind, after which further modulation leads to a new theme in B minor, sketched in descending arpeggios on the guitar. Rapid scales (flute then guitar) herald a reappearance of the rondo (pizzicato violins/guitar arpeggios), this time in G major. In the third and longer episode, yet another idea is proposed by the orchestra and taken up by the guitar alone; pizzicato strings and chirping wood-wind provide a continuation. Eventually, the guitar returns to the rondo theme, this time in flowing semiquavers, then con-tinues without interruption into episode four. At this point a somewhat 'martial' theme is introduced with simulated horn-calls, which the orchestra promptly take up. The episode climaxes with rapid guitar arpeggios, tremolando violins and, after a brief pause, a rapid scale-run into the final presentation of the rondo in D major, by the full orchestra. The coda is brief: octave-leaping arpeggios of the tonic chord (upper strings and woodwind) are followed by a rapid, downward fluttering of the guitar.

The movement ends quietly – almost inconsequentially – but in a way that is wholly appropriate to the subtle sound of the guitar.

Fantasia para un Gentilhombre

With the *Fantasia,* written in 1954, Rodrigo once again proclaims his sense of national history and tradition. Through it, as the title suggests, he pays a tribute to two other great Spanish musicians: Gaspar Sanz (1640–1700), a famous Spanish baroque guitarist whose writings inspired the work, and to Andres Segovia to whom it was dedicated. Segovia was also the soloist at the première of the *Fantasia* in San Francisco in 1958. Before beginning the composition, Rodrigo had told Segovia of his plan. Segovia had approved of the idea but warned Rodrigo of the difficulties of using Sanz's short themes.

Gaspar Sanz was employed by Philip IV of Spain to teach his son, Juan of Austria. Sanz left a three-volume tutor book *Instruccion de Musica sobre la Guitarra español* (1674–97) which contains many settings of popular Spanish dances of the time. During the years spanning the reign of Philip II and Philip IV, music became greatly influenced by popular taste, with the stately dances such as *pavanes* and *gaillards* giving way to less courtly ones whose tunes were usually short, simple and light. Rodrigo selected some of these popular dances from Sanz's writings and used them freely as themes in the *Fantasia.*

Like 'Aranjuez', the *Fantasia* evokes an earlier time through 20th-century language: in Rodrigo's own words, 'My ideal was that if Sanz could hear this work, he would say, "While it isn't exactly me, I can recognise myself" '.

Programme notes

The 17th-century textures of Sanz's settings are clearly audible throughout the *Fantasia,* which is scored for a small orchestra of strings and wind – one each of trumpet, piccolo, flute, oboe and bassoon.

First movement – Villano y Ricercare

The work opens gravely with the *villano,* originally a popular, rustic, sung dance in 4/4 or 'common time', which is marked *adagietto* (slow, but less slow than *adagio*). Rodrigo divides the tune into three strains, to whose repetitions the guitar adds flowing, decorative passages. The first is presented immediately in dialogue between strings and guitar, the second, between strings and wind, the third (an ornamented scale) by the guitar alone. Finally, the first phrase is restated by the whole orchestra, the guitar playing only chords.

After a brief pause, the *Ricercare* follows:

The second movement of 'Fantasia' (title page above) includes a striking adaptation of the fanfare of the Naples cavalry of Sanz's day. Rodrigo uses jangling discords to express the power and bravado of a royal cavalry (right).

in his first book Sanz explains the rules of counterpoint and, as one example, presents a *fugue* (a piece characterized by the interweaving of a fixed number of melodic strands). Rodrigo has elaborated this, working it out at greater length than Sanz did, and retitled it as a *ricercare,* which is a composition of fugal style.

The solo guitar introduces the subject before the orchestra joins in developing it more fully:

The coda that brings the movement to a peaceful end is based on a short derivative phrase, first played by the flute and oboe some bars earlier:

Example 4

The guitar decorates this with undulating *arpeggios.*

Second movement – Españoleta y Fanfare de la Caballeria de Napoles

This movement is based on the *españoleta,* a lilting dance, originating in Italy, also found in Sanz's book. The guitar plays the graceful melody of the dance in 6/8 time, twice over, then after a sequential passage in the orchestra, repeats the melody again. This leads into a discursive (solo) passage that heralds further repetitions by orchestra, first by *pizzicato* (plucked) strings, to which the guitar adds a florid commentary.

Sanz's books contain several curious little fanfares. The one used as the basis of the following interlude is that of the *Caballeria de Napoles* (the Naples

Cavalry). The connection is not as strange as it might seem – Naples was governed by a Spanish viceroy in Sanz's day and Sanz was, for a time, court musician to the Viceroy. Throughout most of the interlude, lower strings and often guitar evoke the sound of trotting horses, dying away at the end to allow the melody of the opening section to return in the full orchestra. Further variations lead to a quiet coda.

Third movement – Danza de las Hachas
The gentle melancholy of the previous movement is swiftly banished by this next 'hatchet dance' marked to be played *allegro con brio* (lively and with vigour). The dance was probably originally a balletic simulation of a combat. Rodrigo says of his setting of it, 'With its great animation, (it) is like a duel between the guitar and the orchestra'.

Fourth movement – Canario
The *canario* was a vigorous dance from the Canary Islands, with energetic leaping and foot-stamping. Sanz's book contains two *canarios,* which Rodrigo juxtaposes in this movement as well as inserting episodes of his own creation.

The guitar begins the movement alone but is soon joined by the orchestra. A brief episode makes much of downward arpeggios which introduce the next syncopated strain of the *canario.* The syncopations are caused by *hemiolas* the rhythmic device wherein two notes are superimposed in a time of three, or three notes in a time of two:

Example 5

Following this, a more extensive episode (of Rodrigo's invention) is initiated by the guitar but at a slower tempo than the previous lively canario sequence.

Example 6

Finally, the original strain and tempo are restored with a display of virtuosity by the guitar which swoops down and up a rapid scale passage, with spiky discords adding a touch of wry humour. The second *canario* arrives via strummed guitar chords but, after some robust treatment, loses momentum. A quiet cuckoo call from the wind brings a response from the guitar, which uses it as the opening to a virtuosic candenza based on the latter part of the first *canario.* Another rapid scale passage leads to the final, joyous summation, brought to an end with another burst of bravura from the guitar and a *tutti* chord from the whole orchestra.

Great interpreters

Odon Alonso (conductor)
Alonso, born in 1925 in Leon, Spain, trained in music from an early age and quickly established that he wanted to be a conductor more than anything else. His first major position was as choral director for the Spanish Radio network towards the end of the 1940s. This post he relinquished in 1952 when he was appointed as conductor of the Spanish National Orchestra, a post he held with distinction for four years. After this successful engagement he moved to the Madrid Philharmonic Orchestra for a number of years before finally taking up with the Spanish Radio and Television Orchestra.

His career has been based for the greater part on Spanish classical music; it is the music he most deeply feels and it is also the music he has most often brought to records. He has recorded works by Turina, Palau and Rodrigo among others, and has often recorded with guitarist Narcisco Yepes. He is regarded today as one of his country's most distinguished interpreters of its national music, and is still busy with recording and live work.

Narcicso Yepes (guitarist)
Yepes is very much a product of Lorca, Southern Spain, where he was born in 1927. He began studying music at Valencia Conservatory at the age of thirteen under the composer and pianist Vincente Ascencio who encouraged him to develop his guitar technique. The Director of the Orquesta Nacional, Ataulfo Argenta, prompted Yepes to move to Madrid after being impressed with his talent, and in 1947 Yepes made his Madrid début before his twentieth birthday, playing Rodrigo's *Concierto de Aranjuez.* Both his and Rodrigo's careers were assured after this

Narcisco Yepes

Edistudio

event, and Yepes became the first guitarist to record the work and, indeed, the first to make his reputation on it. Soon after this, he toured Europe with Argenta, and in 1950 spent a season with Gieseking and Enesco in Paris, studying interpretation with these two masters of music. For the rest of the decade his reputation grew and spread across Europe as the toured more extensively and recorded widely.

Yepes is also a composer/arranger, often involved in film work, his scores include one for *Jeux interdits* (1952) and for *La fille aux yeux d'or* (1961). He spends a great deal of time in researching neglected works from the baroque period, often transcribing them for guitar. He has recorded all of Bach's lute works and has recorded a very wide range of Spanish music together with a vast guitar repertoire. He plays a ten-string guitar, claiming a greater resonance from the instrument and praising its extended range and flexibility which enable him to play more accurate transcriptions.

FURTHER LISTENING
Rodrigo
1 Concierto de Estio for violin (1943)
2 Concierto Andaluz, for four guitars (1967)
3 Concierto Madrigal, for two guitars (1968)

Other Spanish Composers:

Isaac Albeniz (1860–1909)
Piano Works:
1 La Vega (1898)
2 Suite Iberia (Books 1–3)
3 Suite Española, op 47 (1886); Suite Española No. 2 (1889)
Opera:
1 Pepita Jiminez (1896)

Manuel de Falla (1876–1946)
Ballet:
1 El Amor Brujo (1915)
2 El Sombrero des tres picos (1919)
Vocal:
1 La Vida Breve (1904/5) – opera
2 Atlantida (unfinished) (1926–46) – oratorio
Orchestral Music:
1 Noches en las jardines de España (1916)

From Latin America:

Heitor Villa-Lobos (1887–1959): Brazil
Piano:
1 Prole do bebê – Suite No 1 (1918)
2 Prole do bebê – Suite No 2 (1921)
3 Cirandas (16 pieces) (1926)
Guitar:
1 Twelve Etudes, 1929
2 Five Preludes (1940)
Orchestral/Vocal
1 Bachianas Brasilieras Suites, 1–9 (1930–45)
2 Choros (14 works for different instruments) (1920–29)

IN THE BACKGROUND
'Crusade against the godless'

For three bloody years, between 1936 and 1939, Rodrigo's homeland was torn apart by an exceptionally brutal civil war as the forces of Socialism and Fascism fought for supremacy.

The Second Republic of Spain was born in 1931, in an atmosphere of enthusiasm and optimism. King Alfonso XIII, the monarch in name only, had been dismissed without violence, saying as he went into exile, 'Sunday's elections have shown me that I no longer enjoy the love of my people'. Behind lay eight years of military rule, mostly under the leadership of an eccentric and paternalistic dictator, General Primo de Rivera. But economic crisis had led to his fall, and the King, whose prestige suffered along with the regime he had been so closely associated with, had soon followed suit. Now a new liberal government was installed in Madrid.

The constitution adopted by the new republican *cortes* (parliament) was a model of progressive idealism, opposed to everything that Primo de Rivera and the King had stood for, and opposed particularly to the power of the church and army. Instead of a firmly centralized administration, the new government was also in favour of regional autonomy for the independently minded Basque and Catalan populations of Spain.

In the first flush of electoral victory, the *cortes* stripped the Catholic church of much of its property and of control of the schools. But in their zeal, the Republican anti-clericals underestimated some of the practical benefits of Catholicism in traditional Spain. And they overestimated their own capacity to make amends for centuries of social injustice and backwardness.

The new government did not have the resources to replace the religious schools and teachers that it so enthusiastically dispensed with. Worse still, extremist groups were encouraged to take spontaneous illegal action, attacking convents and churches. This kind of violence alienated conservative opinion: even devout Catalans and Basques, who were otherwise in favour of the new government, were deeply disturbed by it.

'An aspirin to cure an appendicitis'

Crucial for the success of the Republican government was a programme of reform in favour of Spain's landless peasants and the workers in her industrial towns. But in implementing it, the government encountered many difficulties. Not least

The ideological struggle between Spain's political Left and Right broke into a civil war which fired international emotions. The poster (left), typical of many that appeared throughout Europe, called on French republicans to join in solidarity with the Spanish workers struggling to preserve their Republic.

was the very nature of the new government itself and its leading figure, Manuel Azana.

The government represented a coalition of different factions ranging from revolutionaries (who wanted a wholesale seizure of property from Spain's ruling class) to more moderate socialists who wanted agrarian reform but were not against private property as such. Because of these differences, the Agrarian Law passed in 1932 was a half measure – labour leader Largo Caballero called it 'an aspirin to cure an appendicitis'.

No-one was happy. The big landlords remained fearful of the government's intentions, and in Andalusia an anarchist movement agitated against the government's half-heartedness. In 1933, in the village of Casas Viejas, a group of disappointed peasants, led by anarchists, staged a pathetic little rising. The government over-reacted: 25 villagers were shot dead in cold blood. The massacre shocked many Republicans, and soon the peasants were joined in their discontent by the industrial workers in the towns.

A great volume of legislation to help working people was introduced by the Republican government, including provision for an eight-hour day and a minimum wage. But again, the government's good intentions were thwarted. In the midst of an international slump, it did not have the funds for reforms. While Spain was suffering from low agricultural prices and widespread unemployment, there was no system of unemployment relief. Soon the government was experiencing bitter opposition from militant workers in industrial Catalonia and was putting down strikes and uprisings with all the ferocity of the military dictatorship that had gone before.

The right mobilizes

While the prisons filled with disaffected supporters of the Second Republic, the reactionary Right began to mobilize. Army officers were prominent among the government's opponents. Staunchly Catholic and, for the most part, monarchists, the army's upper echelons resented the removal of their privileges. They were no longer exempt from the jurisdiction of the civil courts, nor from criticism by the Press.

King Alfonso XIII (left) was the monarchial figurehead allied to the military dictatorship which ruled Spain for eight years before 1931. Following the elections of that year, and the Republican victory, he abdicated. By going, he believed he would avert a civil war. He over-estimated his importance.

Jose Antonio Primo de Rivera (below) son of Spain's military dictator in the time of Alfonso XIII, bitterly resented the inroads made by the new Republican Cortes *(below left) into the powers of church and army. To counter the Republican threat he founded the right-wing Falange Movement in 1933.*

Collection Martin Carrasco, Madrid/Aisa

Aisa

New constitutional right-wing groups such as C.E.D.A. (Confederacion de Derechas Autonomas) sprang up. So, too, did overtly fascist organizations consciously imitating Mussolini and Hitler in Italy and Germany. In Madrid, Jose Antonio Primo de Rivera (son of Primo de Rivera) founded the pro-Nazi Falange movement and eventually fused with another, the Juntas de Ofensiva Nacionel-Sindicalista (J.O.N.S.).

Elections in 1933 ousted the government and, under a new, much more right-wing régime, the *bienio negro* – the two black years – began. Virtually all the progressive legislation of the first administration was repealed, with the status of the Catholic Church being restored and the rights of property reaffirmed.

A deepening crisis

The defeat of the Left was due to internal dissent and a shortage of funds: the progressive parties had not truly lost hold of the majority of the electorate. But when success for the Right increased their confidence and militancy, attitudes on the Left hardened, too. Largo Caballero declared that the Republic was being betrayed, and the Anarchists, already scornful of bourgeois reform, openly revolted. A rising in Saragossa was followed by a wave of strikes throughout Spain, caused by increasing unemployment and social depression. At the same time, the regional parties of Catalonia and the Basque country realized that the new government, unlike the first Republican government, had no time for the issue of their home rule.

In October 1934, an attempt was made to strengthen an already relatively rightist cabinet by including some C.E.D.A. ministers. The atmosphere of crisis intensified and the socialists of the Left revolted. Their rising in Madrid and Barcelona was quickly stamped out. But the militant miners of Asturias could be quelled only by sterner action. The army officer entrusted by the Government with their suppression was Spain's youngest general, Francisco Franco. Already known for his ruthlessness, Franco put down the miners' revolt with such terrifying efficiency that the final death toll was 2000, with twice as many wounded.

In the wake of these events, nearly every prominent leftist leader in Spain was arrested and imprisoned, while a cabinet reshuffle moved the government even more to the right. As the industrial workers smarted at the memory of the Asturias atrocities, the great mass of the rural poor groaned under the government's agrarian policies which maintained the almost feudal, pre-Republican situation. Recurring government scandals involving bribery and corruption helped a coalition of left and moderate political forces – a Popular Front – to win back power in the February 1936 election.

But right-wing monarchists and conservatives were not content to accept defeat.

The prelude to civil war

Spain's new coalition had succeeded because the right-wing government had failed. Once in power, it

In the eyes of the Nationalists, 'Red' Republicanism stood for the destruction of mother Church and traditional values. And the excesses and violence of radical Republicans who burned down churches and murdered clerics, gave fuel to Nationalist propaganda (top left).

Nationalists took up arms against Republicans for the first time in 1932 – in a small revolt centred on Seville (above). But it was a false start to the civil war, which began in earnest in 1936.

Francisco Franco (left), later to become leader of the nationalists, as commander of the Spanish forces in Morocco, 1932. It was from here that he issued his Pronunciamento – a military rising against Republicanism – his bid for power.

Franco's Nationalist forces included right-wing sympathizers from many different nations. Pictured above are Spanish, German, Moroccan and Italian troops taken captive by the Government forces at Guadalajara in 1936.

found it hard to sustain a united front. Most of the politicians were liberal republicans who did not always agree with the more militant politics of the workers who had voted for them. Some two million anarchists, chiefly in Andalusia and Barcelona, despised these politicians as much as those of the *bienio negro.*

Parliamentary bluster and constitutional wrangling were drowned out by the clamour of fighting in the streets. Almost every political organization, right or left, now had its own para-military organization, and they clashed openly. Judges who condemned Falangists to prison were assassinated – so too were journalists who criticized them. Fascists beat up and murdered leftists with impunity. Leftists burned churches and killed civil guards. Factories fell silent during lightning strikes, and estates untouched by the gutless agrarian reform were invaded by revolutionary squatters.

The Pronunciamento
Top army officers began sinister consultations with leading right-wing politicians, the most forceful of whom was Calvo Sotelo (finance minister under

Primo de Rivera). But on 12 July 1936, Sotelo was shot dead by some police officers in retaliation for a murder committed by Falangists. His assassination made the generals bring forward their plans.

The leading figures in this conspiracy against the Second Republic were General Sanjurjo (an exile since leading an unsuccessful coup in 1932), General Mola in the north, General Queipo de Llano in the south, and, of course, Franco. It was Franco who flew from his post in the Canary Islands in a chartered British plane to take command of the army in Morocco, the launching pad for the generals 'crusade' against 'godless', republican Spain.

On 17 July, the army made its declaration of intent, its *pronunciamento,* and on 18 July all the military garrisons in Spain were involved in the rising. In Morocco, where the army's power and influence and popularity were very great, the rebels (or 'nationalists') soon had the upper hand. But to achieve a successful takeover of power, the seat of government, Madrid, had to be captured. To this end, the Generals enlisted the support of like-minded, extreme right wing (Fascist) régimes – Mussolini's Italy and Hitler's Germany.

Archiv für Kunst und Geschichte

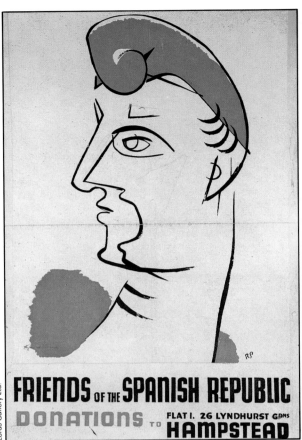

Lords Gallery Ltd.

FRIENDS OF THE SPANISH REPUBLIC

DONATIONS TO FLAT I. 26 LYNDHURST GDNS HAMPSTEAD

Artists and intellectuals in Europe and America threw their weight behind the Republican cause. Writers George Orwell (far left) and Ernest Hemingway both went to fight and returned home to campaign through their writing and radio broadcasting. The artist Roland Penrose designed the appeal-poster, left, to whip up funds.

Early in the war, the Republicans were taken unawares and forced into desperate, pitiable struggles in the streets (right). Gradually the Nationalists experienced set backs as Republican troops became better organized, and won victories of their own, (below) for example, in Seville.

Franco's army had to be transferred from Africa, but the Straits were controlled by ships of the Spanish navy under government control; although the ships' officers were sympathetic to the generals' cause, most of the sailors (who quickly took control) were loyal to the Republic. So 15,000 of Franco's troops were flown to Seville courtesy of Hitler, in German transport planes. The rest were shipped in under escort from the Italian navy and airforce. From the outset, Spain's troubles were no purely internal affair. The civil war which ensued was taken up as a moral and ideological issue by foreigners sympathetic to either the Republic or the generals.

German and Italian military support was to prove crucial to Franco's success, but did not represent a simple gesture of friendship. Spain was to prove a useful training ground for the war machines that were being stockpiled in anticipation of a forthcoming European war. Hitler used Spain to train hs *Luftwaffe,* and the Spanish adventure strengthened his alliance with Mussolini. Mussolini hoped, by his intervention, to strengthen Italy's position in the Mediterranean, and craved the prestige that would accrue from Italian participation in a glorious Nationalist victory.

The Soviet Union sent some fighter planes to the Republican side, and government gold reserves were shipped to Russia to buy arms for Spain. But Russian support was less than that offered by Italy and Germany, and attached to it came Soviet interference, via the Spanish Communist Party, in Republican policy making and internal affairs.

Meanwhile, the Western democracies stood by in the name of a policy of non-intervention. The policy spelled disaster for the Second Republic. The French Popular Front government under Leon Blum was deeply sympathetic . . . but Blum's hands were tied. He was nervous about the strength of his own government and anxious to maintain his alliance with Britain because of the rising menace of Hitler's Germany. The British were totally preoccupied with their own political crisis. The abdication of King Edward VIII absorbed public interest to the exclusion of foreign affairs: the British turned in on themselves, deaf to the appeals of tormented Spain.

Popperfoto

In any event, Prime Minister Baldwin, like other European heads of state, had a tacit policy of non-intervention, a policy which, under Chamberlain, was to culminate in the Munich Pact with Hitler. Like Leon Blum, America's President Roosevelt was sympathetic to the Republic, but he bowed to pressure from his Catholic constituents and did not intervene.

Spanish refugees poured over the Pyrenees, only to be thrown at once into camps; many ended up as prisoners in Nazi Germany when World War II broke out.

Though neighbouring governments hardened their hearts to the plight of the Republic, many individuals felt moved to help. Some arms did find their way to Spain via France, for use by Republicans. Left-wing groups throughout Europe and in America were so

Franco had the support of German and Italian Fascist governments, and their air support (right) largely decided the outcome of the war. In 1937 Hitler's planes razed the Basque town of Guernica to the ground. The atrocity hardened international opposition against Franco. From Hitler's point of view the war was an ideal practice ground for his arsenal.

Popperfoto

concerned for the fate of Spain's Republic that International Brigades were formed to fight in Spain. They consisted mainly of Communist Party members, trade unionists and sympathetic intellectuals – such as George Orwell. Anti-fascist Germans and Italians joined, too. The men of the International Brigades suffered heavy casualties, but helped prevent an early victory by Franco's Nationalists.

The course of the war

In the first six months, the Nationalists carried all before them in the west and south of Spain. Apart from the advantage of surprise and their military strength (Franco's troops included most of the regular officers, the crack Foreign Legionaries and seasoned Moroccan soldiers) the rebels also benefitted from a unified leadership in 'Generalissimo' Franco. Most of his rivials were removed early in the war: Sanjurjo died in a plane crash – (at which point Franco took official command); Queipo de Llano and Mola also met with fatal accidents. By the end of 1936 Franco had installed himself as 'Chief of the Spanish State', at the head of a stern nationalist government sanctioned by the Church.

This government was immediately recognized by

Ciezo de Aragon. Madrid, Archivo Historico Militar/Arxiu Mas

Jesús Martí 'Camino Hacia Francia. 7 Febrero 1939.'/Aisa

Popperfoto

Germany and Italy, and its first legislation, which repealed the Republic's laws on divorce, Catalan autonomy and agrarian reform, left people in no doubt as to the character of the Spain Franco was fighting for.

The generals claimed to be acting in the best interests of Spain, but they seriously underestimated the commitment of the common people to the Republic and democracy, whatever its shortcomings. Now peasants and urban industrial workers ranged themselves against Franco. So too did the Basques and Catalans who stood to lose their regional autonomy. Many ordinary soliders and a few senior army officers – including the celebrated Generals Miaja and Rojo – were pro-Republican.

The Republican cause attracted the support of almost every intellectual in Spain, including the painter Pablo Picasso and the film-maker Luis Buñuel. But the Republican government, now headed by Largo Caballero and composed of socialists, communists and (later) anarchists, lurched from crisis to crisis without ever achieving enough stability to cope. By July 1936 Franco had deprived it of almost half Spain, including the biggest grain-producing areas. Since almost all the state's military resources were on the nationalist side, Republican efforts went mainly towards arming and organizing the people. Real power rested with the labour organizations, which still bickered even in crisis. The Republic's hopes of victory rested with their armed militia.

By the end of 1936, Franco's forces held rather more than half of Spain. They controlled the length of the Portuguese border, a vital supply link. The following year Franco sought to drive a wedge through government territory, cutting Republican Spain in half, to reach Madrid. But he failed. The International Brigades based in Madrid defeated Italian-backed Nationalists at Guadalajara, and after this victory government troops successfully recaptured Teurel. Momentarily thwarted, Franco concentrated on the northern zone of the Basque provinces and the vital natural resources of Asturias. Here he was more successful, and by the summer of 1937, the Basque town of Bilbao had been captured.

The tragedy at Guernica

A small town with a population of 7000, Guernica was the ancient Basque capital. On 26 April 1937, the battlefront was only ten miles away and the town was teeming with refugees and Republican soldiers retreating from the fighting. Though the area had been subjected to air raids before, Guernica itself had not been bombed and there were no air defences of any kind. So when about 43 aircraft – mainly German planes of Hitler's Condor Legion – began saturation bombing with incendiaries and high-explosives, the results were devastating. The centre of the town was left burning and in ruins. Perhaps as many as 1000 men, women and children were killed, with many more injured. There is no evidence that the Germans knew of the historic significance of this market town: it has even been suggested that Franco himself, preoccupied with other military affairs, was

The road to France (left) was choked with Spanish refugees. In April 1938 alone an estimated 20,000 crossed the border, many coming over the mountains through deep snow. France refused to shelter anyone who had taken part in the fighting.

The rebellion of the Nationalist military came fatally late in Madrid. The Republican 'people' anticipated it and besieged the Generals and troops at Montaña Barracks. Eventually, the Republicans fought their way in and killed virtually everyone (above). Indescribable atrocities ensued against soldiers, priests, nuns and anyone remotely well-off, which shame the memory of the Republican Madrileños – though they themselves were finally butchered by Nationalists in much larger numbers.

furious when he heard of the horrific raid. The massacre shocked the world and precipitated an international controversy. Guilt and anxiety about the repercussions made the nationalists and Germans try to conceal what they had done. They claimed the destruction had been the work of Basque propagandists, but eye-witness reports were appearing in newspapers in a dozen countries.

The Pope, however, chose to ignore Guernica as if it had never happened. The Germans blamed bad bomb sights, then admitted that it had in fact been an experiment in the effectiveness of saturation bombing. The Nationalists said, 'We bombed it, and bombed it and bombed it, and *bueno* why not?' In terms of the massacres that took place elsewhere, it has even to be thought of as 'peanuts'.

It was a ferocious war, stained by atrocities on both sides. Many of the early Nationalist gains were made only after the wholesale slaughter of dissidents. Enraged Republicans and anti-clericals took summary vengeance on members of the upper classes. Churches were gutted and nearly 5000 priests killed in cold blood. By 1937 most Spaniards, if only to protect their lives, had chosen sides.

To be in the wrong place at the wrong time was fatal. The poet and dramatist Garcia Lorca was shot dead by Nationalist troops in 1936 – because he was an intellectual, he was automatically deemed an enemy. His body was never found. José Antonio de Primo Rivera, founder of the Falange movement, perished in a Republican gaol. Despite the great heroism shown – that of the besieged Nationalists at Alcazar, for instance, or of the Republican defenders of Madrid – it was a war that shamed both sides.

An uncompromising victory

Slowly but surely the Nationalists, by superiority of military skill and armaments, gained the upper hand. By August 1938, backed by as many as 100,000 Italian troops and with efficient German equipment, Franco had broken through government territory and reached the sea. The Republican government was frustrated in its attempts to gain supplies from friendly countries, and when the Russians cut off their limited aid in 1939, its death knell was tolled.

After repeated heavy bombing, Barcelona fell in 1939 and Madrid capitulated. Racked by intrigue and internal dissent, the forces of the legitimate government collapsed.

On March 31st, Portugal formally recognized the new Spain. Meanwhile, at ports along the Mediterranean coast, hundreds of frightened Republicans, unable to afford passage on outward-bound ships, began committing suicide rather than face the Fascist régime.

General Franco insisted on unconditional surrender, and his victory was not magnanimous. After the fall of Madrid, Republican sympathizers were executed in their thousands. According to one conservative estimate, as many people were put to death by the winning side *after* the civil war as had been killed *during* it.

Altogether, Spain's ordeal cost a million lives and caused incalculable material damage. It was a clash not just between Socialism and Fascism, but between all the forces in Spain that believed in parliamentary democracy and social reform and the forces that clung to the traditional order. Recovery from this extremely bitter war was destined to be slow, for World War II began just as Spain's trauma ended. She was left to rebuild her future as best she could under a new master. Franco disappointed his sponsors by not entering the war on their side, but he survived them, remaining in control of Spain until 1975.

In January 1937, Malaga was a staunch Republican stronghold. In one week in February, Nationalist forces seized the town. The following week 4,000 prisoners were shot, most without trial. The Nationalist salute was common in Malaga that week (above).

Contemporary composers

Arnold Bax
(1883-1953)

Born in London, Bax studied piano at the Royal Academy of Music. His earliest works were symphonic poems based upon Celtic legends. He spent the year 1910 in Russia; the famous Russian impresario Sergei Diaghilev later produced his ballet, *The Truth About the Russian Dancers*. He wrote seven symphonies and numerous other works in a rich, neo-Romantic style. Bax also wrote short stories and poetry. He was named Master of the King's Music in 1942.

Arthur Bliss
(1891-1975)

Born in London, Bliss studied music with both Ralph Vaughan Williams and Gustav Holst. His early works were experimental; after 1920, however, he turned to a more mainstream, classical style in his choral works and symphonies. He wrote three ballets, including the English repertory classic, *Checkmate*, and also composed music for films and television. He was named Master of the Queen's Music in 1953.

Frederick Delius
(1862-1934)

Born in London, Delius worked for his father's manufacturing firm and managed an orange grove in Florida before deciding to study music. He attended the Leipzig Conservatory in 1886; two years later, he moved to Paris and began to compose in earnest. Among his distinctive works were six operas and several choral and orchestral works. Despite the onset of blindness and paralysis in the early 1920s, he continued to write; his mastery of the late Romantic style did much to revive English music at the turn of the century.

Manuel de Falla
(1876-1946)

Falla was born in Cádiz and studied composition in Madrid. He moved to Paris in 1907, where he published his first compositions and met Ravel, Dukas and Debussy. He returned to Madrid in 1914 and soon gained international fame for his colourful and evocative ballet scores and piano concertos. His later works, including a chamber opera and a concerto, showed a more neo-classical style. He moved to Argentina in 1939, where he worked on a large cantata; after his death in 1946, a pupil of Falla's completed the work.

Gustav Mahler
(1860-1911)

Mahler was the last of the great symphonic composers to be based in Vienna. He was born in Moravia and, encouraged by his family, was sent to the Vienna Conservatory in 1875. He struggled to support himself as a composer, and decided to take up con-ducting. Over the following years, he rose to the top of his profession to become artistic director of the Vienna State Opera in 1897. As a conductor he was remarkably innovative, though subject to controversy; but as a composer, his works were largely ignored until some fifty years after his death. Today, his ten symphonies are seen as works of true genius, and Mahler is recognized as a powerful influence on music in a time of great transition.

Ralph Vaughan Williams
(1872-1958)

Vaughan Williams, born in Gloucestershire, England, began to compose at the age of six. He studied composition at the Royal College of Music and also earned degrees in both history and music at Cambridge University. He used England's folk song tradition and English musical styles, particularly those of the 16th century, in his works, which included symphonies and several choral and orchestral works. He continued to compose until his death in 1958.

William Walton
(1902-1983)

Born in Lancashire, England, Walton taught himself composition. He studied music at Oxford University, but failed by one examination to earn his degree. He was unofficially adopted by the Sitwell family and composed *Façade* for chamber ensemble in 1923 to accompany a poetry reading by Edith Sitwell. Several orchestral works followed, which established his reputation as a boldly creative composer. He also wrote music for the theatre and for films. He was given a knighthood in 1951.

Bibliography

Del Mar, N. *Richard Strauss: A Critical Commentary on his Life and Works*. Cornell University Press (Ithaca, 1986).

Holst, I. *Gustav Holst: A Biography*. Oxford University Press (New York, 1988).

Holst, I. *The Music of Gustav Holst*. Oxford University Press (New York, 1986).

Jefferson, A. *Der Rosenkavalier*. Cambridge University Press Handbooks (New York, 1986).

Kennedy, M. *Portrait of Elgar*. Oxford University Press (New York, 1987).

Kennedy, M. *Richard Strauss*. Rowman (Totowa, 1983).

McVeagh, D. *Edward Elgar: His Life and Music*. Hyperion (New York, 1984).

Mason, D. *Romantic Composers*. Greenwood (Westport, 1970).

Reed, W. *Elgar as I Knew Him*. Oxford University Press (New York, 1989).

Young, P. *Elgar OM: The Study of a Musician*. Greenwood (Westport, 1987).

Index